THE CARVED CUPBOARD

AMY LE FEUVRE

1st WORLD
LIBRARY
Literary Society

The Carved Cupboard

Amy Le Feuvre

© 1st World Library, 2009
PO Box 2211
Fairfield, IA 52556
www.1stworldlibrary.com
First Edition

LCCN: 2009923343

Softcover ISBN: 978-1-4218-8808-8
Hardcover ISBN: 978-1-4218-8907-8
eBook ISBN: 978-1-4218-8709-8

Purchase *"The Carved Cupboard"*
as a traditional bound book at:
www.1stWorldLibrary.com/purchase.asp?ISBN=978-1-4218-8808-8

1st World Library is a literary, educational organization
dedicated to:

- Creating a free internet library of downloadable ebooks

- Hosting writing competitions and offering book publishing
scholarships.

Interested in more 1st World Library books? contact:
literacy@1stworldlibrary.com
Check us out at: www.1stworldlibrary.com

1ˢᵗ World Library Literary Society

Giving Back to the World

"If you want to work on the core problem, it's early school literacy."

- James Barksdale, former CEO of Netscape

"No skill is more crucial to the future of a child, or to a democratic and prosperous society, than literacy."

- Los Angeles Times

"Literacy... means far more than learning how to read and write... The aim is to transmit... knowledge and promote social participation."

- UNESCO

"Literacy is not a luxury, it is a right and a responsibility. If our world is to meet the challenges of the twenty-first century we must harness the energy and creativity of all our citizens."

- President Bill Clinton

"Parents should be encouraged to read to their children, and teachers should be equipped with all available techniques for teaching literacy, so the varying needs and capacities of individual kids can be taken into account."

- Hugh Mackay

CONTENTS

CHAPTER I

A SUPPLANTER

'For troubles wrought of men,
Patience is hard.'
—*J. Ingelow*

The firelight shone upon a comfortably-furnished drawing-room in one of the quiet London squares, and upon four girlish figures grouped around a small tea-table. Agatha Dane, the eldest, sat back in her chair with a little wrinkle of perplexity upon her usually placid brow. Rather plump and short of stature, with no pretensions to beauty, there was yet something very attractive in her bright open countenance; and she was one to whom many turned instinctively for comfort and help.

Gwendoline, who sat next her, and was doing most of the talking, was a tall, slight, handsome girl, with dark eyes that flashed and sparkled with animation as she spoke, and there was a certain stateliness of carriage that made some of her acquaintances term her proud.

Clare was toying absently with her spoon and tea-cup; she was listening, and occasionally put in a word, but her thoughts were evidently elsewhere. She had not the determination in her face that was Gwendoline's characteristic; and perhaps the varying expressions passing over it, and so transparent to those who knew her, formed her chief charm. There was a wistfulness in her dark blue eyes, and a look of expectation that one longed to see fulfilled; and her dreamy preoccupied manner often made her friends wonder if she spent all her time in dreamland.

Elfrida sat on the hearth-rug with her sunny hair glistening in the firelight. She was the youngest and prettiest of the four, and had only just returned from Germany that same day. It was her eager questioning that was making them all linger over their tea.

'But I don't understand,' she said, a little impatiently. 'How does Cousin James happen to be here at all? Aunt Mildred never cared for him. She said last year when I was home that he was a regular screw, and that he only came on a visit to save his housekeeping bills. Now I come back and find dear Aunt Mildred gone, and he in full possession of our home, ready to turn us out to-morrow, you say! Aunt Mildred always told us we should never want after her death.'

'We shall not actually do that,' said Agatha quietly, 'for she has left us a legacy each, which will at any rate keep the wolf from the door.'

'But hasn't she left us Dane Hall? She always said she would.'

'No; a codicil to that will has been added since James has been here.'

'Yes; he has managed it beautifully,' put in Gwendoline, with scorn in her tone. 'He came down here directly he heard she

Amy Le Feuvre

was ill, and established himself in the dressing-room next to hers. Clare has been away, but Agatha and I were virtually shut out of the sick-room from the time he entered the house. He got a trained nurse; said Agatha was worn out, and must rest; and told Nannie she was too old and too near-sighted to be left alone with her mistress. The poor old soul has been weeping her eyes out since! Then he took advantage of Aunt Mildred's state of weakness, and worried and coaxed her into making this unjust codicil. All in his favour, of course; I don't believe poor aunt knew what she was doing. And we shall have to shift for ourselves now. I hope he will enjoy his unrighteous possessions. I—I hate him!'

'What are we going to do?'

'Well,' said Agatha, rousing herself, 'we have been talking over matters together. You see, we can be independent of each other if we choose, for we are all of age, and have each about 100 pounds a year, besides what the sale of this house will bring us.'

'Oh, she left us this house, did she? Then why can't we go on living here?'

'The lease terminates at the end of this year, and we have not the income to keep it up. Why, Elfie, a town house like this is ruinous for people of small means! I feel anxious for us to have a home together somewhere, even if we have to go into the country for it; but, of course, I would not influence any of you to side with me against your inclinations.'

'It would be an establishment of old maids; single women, shall we say? It doesn't sound very nice, buried away in the country.'

Elfie spoke dubiously; then Gwen broke in, 'Well, if Clare is wise, she will marry soon. I'm sure two years' engagement ought to be long enough in all conscience to satisfy her!'

Clare's soft cheeks flushed a little.

'Hugh is going out to Africa, you know, with a survey party. We could not settle till after that. He is quite of the same mind as I am on that point!'

'Do you like the country plan, Gwen?' asked Elfie.

'Yes, I think I do. I am personally sick of town. A suburban life would be intolerable, and we have all resources enough to prevent us from stagnating.'

Elfie gave a little sigh.

'You don't know how I was looking forward to a London season. I have been in Germany ever since I left school, studying music. And now what is the good of it? I shall be out of touch with it entirely.'

'Would you like to stay in town for a little?' asked Agatha sympathetically. 'We could easily arrange for you to board with some nice people somewhere.'

'No, I will come with you, and see how it works. I suppose we shall not be banished from London for ever? We can sometimes come up for a short stay?'

'Oh yes, I think so. We have not settled where to live yet, but we have been looking through some house agents' lists, and Gwen is full of plans, as usual.'

'You would be badly off without me to keep you all alive,' said Gwen laughing. 'If I were by myself, I would like nothing better than a caravan or a house-boat; but that wouldn't suit all of us.'

'Not me,' said Clare, with a little grimace of disgust.

'Oh, it is a shame!' exclaimed Elfie, springing up, and walking up and down in her excitement; 'how dare Cousin James behave so treacherously! Can't we dispute the will? Can't we go to law?'

'It is useless to think of such a thing. We can prove nothing. He is a man, and has had a jealous feeling of us all our lives. Now fortune has favoured him, and he is glorying in his prosperity. He is rightly named James, or Jacob, for he is a base supplanter!'

'Will you give me a cup of tea?'

Gwen started at the voice following her hot outburst so quickly, and Elfie stopped her hurried walk, and turned a little defiantly towards the new-comer.

Mr. James Dane was a quiet-looking, sprucely-dressed man of over forty years of age. He seated himself with the greatest equanimity in the midst of the group, and Agatha in silence poured him out a cup of tea, and handed it to him.

'I am afraid I have interrupted a very animated discussion,' he said blandly. 'I suppose you are arranging future plans. Of course, you cannot well remain here. Would you like me to take any steps about the sale for you? I shall be a week longer in town.'

'Mr. Watkins will arrange all that for us, thank you,' replied Agatha quietly.

'Oh, very well. Why, Elfrida, I never noticed you! Just come back from Germany, have you? It seems to have suited your health. You are looking quite bonny.'

'I don't feel so,' was the blunt reply; 'it is not a very happy home-coming!'

'No, of course not. But, as my wife was saying this morning, you girls can only have pleasant memories of your dear aunt, who did so much for you all when she was alive. I remember when first you all arrived from India, and she was in such an anxious state of bewilderment at the thought of the charge of four orphan children, my mother said to her, "Oh, well, Mildred, if you are good enough to educate them, they will naturally do something later to relieve you of the burden of maintaining them." And my wife and I have been so surprised at your all continuing to look upon her house as your rightful home. I suppose in the goodness of her heart she insisted upon it. Still, nowadays, young ladies are so independent, and have such a wide scope for their talents, that we quite expected to hear you were supporting yourselves, after the liberal education that you have received.'

There was dead silence after this speech, which Gwen broke at last, and her tone was haughtiness itself.

'As you have met with such success in your visit here, Cousin James, you could at least afford to be generous towards us. You have one mercy to be thankful for, and that is, that we never have, and never shall, look to you to maintain us!'

And then she left the room, shutting the door behind her with a rather ungentle hand. Mr. Dane smiled, passed his cup to be refilled, and then turned to Clare.

'I suppose your marriage will be hastened now, will it not? When is the happy day to be?'

'I will let you know when it is settled,' was the quiet reply.

'Come upstairs with me, Clare, and see Nannie,' said Elfie impetuously; 'I haven't been near her yet, dear old thing!'

The two girls quitted the room together, and with a little sigh Agatha settled herself down to a *tete-a-tete* with her cousin.

'You girls have all assumed such aggressive demeanours towards me, that I really hardly know if you will take any advice from me. It is exceedingly foolish to adopt such airs. No doubt you are disappointed in not being the sole heiresses of our aunt, but you ought not to have expected it for a moment. She had for a long time regretted making that rash will, which was drawn up when her heart was full of pity for your penniless condition. Only, being in such robust health, she always put off doing it until this last sad illness of hers. Where do you think of settling?'

'We have not made up our minds.'

'Have you heard from your brother lately? Is he doing better than he was? It is such a mistake for a young fellow to think he will make his fortune in the Colonies nowadays. I only hope you may not find him thrown on your hands soon.'

'Walter is doing very well, thank you. There is no chance of his coming back to England for a good long time.'

'I have been wondering whether you would like to settle somewhere near London. I have some house property at Hampstead, and could let you have a small villa there at a very reasonable rent. Of course, understand, this is entirely because I should like to give you any help that I can.'

At this Agatha could not help smiling.

'It is very kind of you, but we have decided to live in the country.'

'I am surprised. Have you ever tried a country life in the winter? I am afraid you will find it a great failure. And, remember, unprotected females, choosing an isolated position, run the risk of being robbed. If you do go to the country, be sure and get a house near others. Well, I must be going. Say good-bye to the others for me. I shall look in again on you before long, and if you want me, you know my club. Your cousin Helen has left town, and I shall be taking a trip to the Continent with her very soon.'

He rose, shook hands politely, and directly the door closed upon him, Agatha hastened to find her sisters.

She knew where to look for them. In a small room at the end of the passage past the best bedrooms, Nannie would now be taking her afternoon cup of tea. She had been with them all since they were quite tiny children; had brought them over from India after their parents' death, and had been kept in Miss Dane's service ever since—first as their nurse, then as housekeeper, when they no longer needed her care.

She was an old woman now, crippled with rheumatism; but she was a bright and happy Christian, and had a good influence upon all who came in contact with her. It had been already arranged that she was to go into an alms-house when the house was sold, and Miss Dane had left her a small legacy, so that her future was provided for. Agatha's face as she opened the door was a troubled one. She saw the old woman in her easy chair by the fire; Gwen and the two younger ones making themselves comfortable round her; and all were talking freely to her of what had passed downstairs.

'Come along, Agatha; has he gone?'

'Yes,' was the reply; 'and I have come to Nannie to be soothed. All the way upstairs I have been saying to myself, "Fret not thyself, because of him who prospereth in his way." But it is hard to see his self-complacency.'

'Poor old thing! When Agatha is disturbed, it must be something indeed! Here is a seat. Nannie has been scolding us, and now she shall scold you.'

CHAPTER II

FOUR VERSES

'In preparing a guide to immortality, Infinite Wisdom gave not a dictionary, nor a grammar, but a Bible—a book of heavenly doctrine, but withal of earthly adaptation.'

—*J. Hamilton*

The old woman looked through her glasses at her four nurslings with a loving eye; then she said very quietly, 'I have been hearing all about your plans, Miss Agatha, and I'm thinking you have shown your wisdom in keeping a home together. Forgive my plain speaking. I know 'tis an age for young ladies to make homes for themselves, anywhere and everywhere, but unless a woman is married, 'tis a risky undertakin'! I've been inclined to fret that my working days are over, for dearly would I like to have gone with you, and done what I could to make you comfortable; but 'tis the Lord's will, and my age and helplessness doesn't prevent me from prayin' for you all! You have the same psalm in your mind, Miss Agatha, that I have been readin' and studyin' this afternoon. I would dearly like to give you each a verse out of it, if you won't take offence.'

Amy Le Feuvre

'We're in for one of Nannie's preaches!' said Gwen, laughing, as she placed a large-print Bible before her old nurse; 'but we shan't have a chance of many more, so we promise to be attentive!'

'Ay, dear Miss Gwen, it isn't a preach! How often you come up here to have a cup o' tea to refresh your bodies! and 'tis a bit of refreshment to your souls that I'm now makin' so bold as to offer.' Nannie turned over the pages of her beloved Bible with a reverent hand, then she looked across at Agatha.

'My dear Miss Agatha, there are four verses here, with a command and a promise. I should like to give you each one to think of, through all the troubles and trials that may come to you. Will you mark it in your own Bibles, and live it out, remembering it was Nannie's verse for you, so that when I'm dead and gone you may still have the comfort and teachin' of it?'

Agatha was touched by the old woman's solemn earnestness.

'Yes, Nannie, give it to me, and I will try and put it "into practice."'

Nannie's voice rang out in the dusky firelit room, as she repeated, more from memory than by sight,—

'Trust in the Lord, and do good; so shalt thou dwell in the land, and verily thou shalt be fed!'

'Thank you, Nannie,' said Agatha after a pause, 'I will look it up and remember it.'

'Now mine, please,' said Gwen, looking over the old woman's shoulder. 'Is it the next verse for me?'

'No, my dear, I think not. It seems to me that this must be the Lord's word to you: "Commit thy way unto the Lord, trust also in Him, and He shall bring it to pass."'

'You have given me that because you think I like choosing my own way through life, now haven't you?'

'Maybe I have. Choosing our own ways and goin' in them always bring trouble in the end. Now, Miss Clare, your verse is the beginning of the one Miss Agatha was sayin': "Rest in the Lord, and wait patiently for Him"; and, Miss Elfie, this is for you, "Delight thyself also in the Lord, and He shall give thee the desires of thine heart."'

'And I am the only one that has got a command without a promise,' said Clare reproachfully.

Nannie looked at Clare, then at her big Bible again.

'You have a promise further on, Miss Clare, "Those that wait upon the Lord, they shalt inherit the earth."'

'Ah, Nannie, that is too big a promise to realize. If it was to inherit Dane Hall now!'

'My dear, since you were a little wee child, you have always been looking for something big. You will inherit more from God Almighty, if you wait for Him, than ever you could inherit without Him!'

There was silence for a few minutes; then Gwen said, trying to speak lightly, 'We shan't forget your verses, Nannie; and though I'm afraid none of us will ever grow into such a saint as yourself, it won't be for want of an example before us. Now may we turn to business? Jacob has gone, and we must bestir ourselves. I have cut out an advertisement from the

Morning Post, which I think sounds tempting. And as Agatha seems so slow in making up her mind, I think I shall take the train to-morrow morning and go and inspect the place myself. Doesn't it sound as if it ought to suit us? "To Let. An old-fashioned cottage residence, four bedrooms, two attics, three reception-rooms, well-stocked fruit and vegetable garden. Owner called abroad suddenly; will let on reasonable terms!"'

'Where is it?' asked Elfie.

'Hampshire. I wrote to the agent who advertises, and he said the rent would be about 40 pounds. It is close to some pine woods, and only three miles from a town. It sounds nice, I think; at any rate, it is worth seeing about.'

'Do you like old-fashioned cottage residences?' said Clare very dubiously; 'they always remind me of rotten floors, rats and mice, and damp musty rooms.'

I hate modern villas,' retorted Gwen, 'with gimcrack walls and smoky chimneys and bad drainage! This has an old-world sound. Let us, if we live out of town, choose an Arcadia, with nothing to remind us of the overcrowded suburbs. Are you willing I should go, Agatha, and come back and report the land?'

Yes,' said Agatha; 'better you should do it than I, for what suits you will suit me, but what would suit me might not suit you. We will talk it over when you come back.'

And so it was settled; and after an early breakfast next day, Gwen started on her quest.

She did not come back till between seven and eight o'clock in the evening, and seemed so tired that Agatha insisted upon her eating a good dinner before she gave an account of herself. Then, rested and refreshed, she came into the drawing-room and settled herself in a comfortable chair by the fire to give her experiences.

'I really think it will do,' she began. 'I arrived at the station about twelve o'clock, and walked out the three miles, to see what the country was like. Brambleton is a clean, empty little town, with no one in the streets but a few tottering old men and children, a few good shops, and there is a market every Friday. I walked along the high road for a couple of miles, then turned up a lane with a ragged piece of common at the end of it, passed one or two nice houses standing back in their own grounds, a little country church with parsonage adjoining in the orthodox fashion, a cluster of thatched cottages, and finally came to the "cottage residence."'

'Is it in a village street?' asked Agatha.

'No, not exactly. It is in a side road leading to a farm. It is a low white house with a great box hedge hiding it from the road, and a stone-flagged path leading up to the door. A blue trellis verandah runs right round it, which I rather liked, and a row of straw bee-hives in front delighted me. There was an old woman in charge, who showed me all over, and talked unceasingly.'

'Now describe the rooms exactly,' said Elfie eagerly; 'and did the house smell musty and damp?'

'No, I shouldn't say it was at all damp; of course rooms that have been shut up always seem fusty and close. It is a little place; you must not think the rooms are anything like this. On one side of the door is a long low room, the width of the house, with a window at each end; the other side of the passage there are two smaller rooms; the kitchens, etcetera,

Amy Le Feuvre

lie out at the back; and the stairs go up in the middle of the passage. Four fair-sized bedrooms are above, and the two attics are quite habitable. The back of the house has the best view; it overlooks a hill with a cluster of pines, and woods in the distance. Fields are round it, but the back garden has a good high brick wall, with plenty of fruit trees, and all laid out as a kitchen garden. The front piece is in grass, with a dear old elm in the corner.'

I don't like the sound of the box hedge,' said Agatha thoughtfully; 'it seems so shut in, and very lonely, I should say.'

'Of course we shall not have many passers-by, except the carters to and from the farm; but if you are in the country, what can you expect? We can cut down the hedge. I like the place myself, and it is in good repair, for the owner has only just left it. I must tell you about him, for there is quite a story about him. Old Mrs. Tucker was his cook. He is an eccentric widower, and has a brother with a lot of property in the neighbourhood. He spends his time in carving, painting, and writing about old manuscripts. That is one thing you will like, Clare; all the doors and cupboards in the house are carved most beautifully, even the low window sills, and mantelpieces. About four months ago he had a dreadful quarrel with his brother, and told Mrs. Tucker that he was going abroad till his temper cooled. He stored all his furniture, and said he would let the house, but only to a yearly tenant, as he might wish to return again. That is the disadvantage of the house; but I think he will not be in a hurry to return. There is an old carved cupboard let into the wall in the room which was his study, and this he has left locked, and wishes any tenant to understand that it is not to be opened. They take the house under this condition.'

'A Bluebeard's cupboard,' said Clare delightedly. 'Why, this is most interesting. I am longing to take the house now.'

'That is indeed a woman's speech,' said a voice behind her, and a tall broad-shouldered man laid his hand gently on her shoulder.

Clare turned round, with a pretty pink colour in her cheeks.

'Oh, Hugh, is it you? Come and sit down, and hear about the cottage we meditate taking. Gwen is our business man, and seems to have found just the place we wanted.'

Captain Knox took a seat by his betrothed, and was soon hearing about it all. Then after it was discussed afresh, and he agreed that it might prove suitable, the other girls slipped away to the inner drawing-room, and left the young couple alone.

Clare's wistful dreaminess had vanished now, and she was bright and animated.

'I believe you girls are rejoicing in your sudden downfall,' said Captain Knox at length; 'I hear no moans now over your lost fortunes. It is the outside world that is pitying you. "Those poor girls," I hear on all sides, "after the very marked way in which old Miss Dane told everybody they would be heiresses at her death. It is most incomprehensible."'

It is no laughing matter, Hugh,' said Clare gravely. 'We are going to try and make the best of it; but when we think of James, our blood boils!'

'Well, darling, you will never know actual want, that is my comfort. How I wish I could offer you a home now! but I have been advised so strongly to go with this party that I feel I ought not to refuse. It will only be a matter of six months, I hope, and then I shall take you away from your country retreat altogether.'

'I sometimes wish—' Clare stopped.

'Well, what?'

'I was going to say I wish you were not in the army, but that is wrong. I do so much prefer a settled home to the incessant change in the service.'

Captain Knox's brows clouded a little, for he was a keen soldier, and was devoted to his corps, which was the Royal Engineers.

'But, Clare, I have heard you say before that you do not care for a gay town life, nor a quiet country one; so what do you like?'

'I don't know what I like,' she said, laughing; 'generally it is what I haven't got. Don't mind my grumblings. I shall be so tired of the country, and the dull monotony of it all, by the time you come back, that I shall fly to you with open arms, and entreat you to take me into the very midst of garrison gaiety.'

Captain Knox smiled, though he still looked perplexed. Clare's moods, and contradictions of humour, were inexplicable to a man of his frank, straightforward nature. Yet she was so sweetly penitent after a fit of discontent, and so delightful in her waywardness, that he only loved her the more, and found, as so many others do, that woman is a problem that few masculine brains can solve.

Whilst the two lovers were enjoying their *tete-a-tete*, Elfie had crept upstairs to see Nannie, and a gravity had settled on her usually sunny face as she entered her nurse's room.

'Have you come for a chat, Miss Elfie?' inquired the old

woman, brightening at the sight of her.

'Yes, Nannie. I have been thinking over my verse that you gave me. I can't get it out of my head. It is a very lovely one, but very difficult to put into practice, I should think.'

'Why, surely, no, my dear! And for you 'tis easier than most.'

'That is because I always say I find it is easy to be happy. But, Nannie, delighting oneself in the Lord is a very different thing.'

'Ay, but the lark that rises with his song, and the flowers that turn their faces to the sun, or soft refreshing showers, don't find it difficult to delight themselves in the air and sunshine. I think, Miss Elfie, you are one of the Lord's dear children, are you not?'

Elfie's face flushed; then sitting down in a low chair, she rested her head against Nannie's knees.

'Yes,' she said softly. 'I told you how different everything had been with me when last I was home, Nannie. That German governess was such a help to me. But what I feel is this: I enjoy everything in life so; it all seems so bright and sunny to me, that I feel the pleasure I take in everything may be such a snare. I ought to have my enjoyment in the Lord apart from it all. And I sometimes ask myself if I could be happy shut up in a prison cell, away from all I love, and—and I almost think I couldn't. Nannie smiled.

'You are a foolish child. Do you think the Lord loves to put His children in miserable circumstances and keep them there? Your youth and your gladness and your hopes are all gifts from Him. He loves to see us happy. Doesn't the sun, and the brightness, and all the lovely bits o' nature, come

Amy Le Feuvre

straight from Him? He didn't make London with its smoke and fog and misery, 'tis us that have done that.'

'But I like London,' put in Elfie. 'I love the shops and the people and the bustle, and at first I didn't like the idea of the country at all, but now I am beginning to.'

'Wherever you may be, Miss Elfie, delight yourself in your surroundings, unless they be sinful; but be sure o' this, you can delight yourself in the Lord in the midst of it all, and have no need to separate Him from all your innocent joys. Doesn't your verse say as much? Will the Lord take all that is pleasant away from you, if you do His command? No; "He will give thee the desires of thine heart." Could you want more proof of His love? You may later on in life have another lesson to learn, but 'twill come easier then, and you'll be able to say with Habakkuk, "Although everything else fails, yet I will rejoice in the Lord."'

Elfie was silent. Then she got up and kissed her old nurse.

'You're an old saint; you always do me such a world of good. I think you have given me the best verse of them all, and I will try and make it my motto. Now I must go. I only ran up to have a peep at you.'

CHAPTER III

A COUNTRY HOME

'If thou would'st read a lesson that will keep
Thy heart from fainting, and thy soul from sleep,
Go to the woods and hills. No tears
Dim the sweet look that Nature wears.'

—Longfellow

The day had come when the four sisters took their leave of London. The sale had taken place, as they only took enough furniture for their small house, and Nannie had taken a tender and sad farewell of her charges.

'I feel,' said Gwen, after they had watched her driven away in a cab with all her little belongings, 'that Nannie does not expect to see any of us again. She has given us her dying blessing, like Jacob did to his sons. I wonder if her verses will prove prophetic.'

Captain Knox went with them to the station, to see the last of Clare. He cheered her up by saying he would run down and see them before he went abroad, and the sisters were all doing their best to be cheerful. They had sent down two

Amy Le Feuvre

young maids the day before to get things comfortable, and both Agatha and Gwen had been backwards and forwards arranging their furniture, so that they did not feel they were going into a comfortless house.

'I always like everything new,' asserted Elfie. 'I feel quite excited to see what it will be like.'

'I think it is a dear little place,' Agatha said. 'I am sure we shall be happy there.'

But their arrival at Brambleton station was in the midst of steady, driving rain, and a wind that threatened instant destruction to open umbrellas. A fly was found, and they were soon driving along the country road, all distant scenery being obliterated by mist and wet. Clare's spirits sank at once.

'What a dreadful day, and what miserable country!'

'I hope the house won't be damp,' Agatha said anxiously.

Then Gwen laughed.

'Oh, for pity's sake, don't all begin to croak! We do have wet days in London. If Jane and Martha have done their work properly, we shall soon forget the wet when we are inside.'

Slowly the fly lumbered along, and darkness had set in when they at last reached their new home.

Mrs. Tucker, who was keeping the maids company, came bustling to the door, and when they saw the cheerful little dining-room with its blazing fire and well-spread table for their evening meal, the wind and wet outside were forgotten.

Elfie ran in and out of the rooms, delighted with the quaintness of it all, and Clare grew quite enthusiastic over the carved wood decorations.

'He must be an artist,' she exclaimed. 'How could he go off and leave it all to strangers?'

The rooms, though lacking as yet in all the details of comfort, were quite habitable, and the late dinner was a merry meal.

'We shall be a community of women, with no opportunities of getting away from one another occasionally; that is what I object to,' said Clare, leaning back in her chair, and looking at her sisters rather meditatively. 'If we quarrel, it will be dreadful, and I am perfectly certain we shall never agree on every point.'

'*You* will not on *any* point,' said Gwen, a little drily.

'We have the country round us,' put in Elfie, 'and there must be some people to know; it is only just at first we shall be shut up to ourselves, I expect.'

'As to the people, there will be the villagers, of course,' said Gwen briskly; 'but we needn't count upon many friends in our own class of life. The big houses round here won't be desirous of the acquaintance of four unknown females with a very small income.'

'I always thought,' said Elfie, 'that country villages contained a clergyman and family, a doctor, and a squire. Isn't that the case here?'

'No; this is a kind of suburb of Brambleton. There is a vicarage, but I don't know anything about the clergyman.'

Amy Le Feuvre

'Well, I hope we shan't all die of the dumps,' said Clare, shivering slightly, as a fresh blast of wind howled and shrieked in the old chimney.

'Oh, that dreadful wind, how I hate it! It seems like a bad omen to have such a welcome when we get here.'

'Rubbish! Go to bed, if you don't like it, and put your head under the clothes. Of course we notice the wind more in the country because of the trees.'

Clare did not get much sympathy from her sisters, and she soon left them and went up to her bedroom. There was a bright fire burning, and some of her own pretty things were already being unpacked by the busy Jane, who was perhaps more attached to her than to any of the others.

'Captain Knox thinks her the best of the bunch,' said she in confidence to Martha, when on the subject of 'our young ladies,' 'and so do I—Miss Agatha is rather commonplace, to my mind, though she is a good mistress, and Miss Gwendoline is always catching up one and taking one's breath away. Miss Elfrida is very pleasant, but she's always the same. Now Miss Clare's never two days alike; she's that gentle and appealin' sometimes, that she makes me love her, and then she's miles away in the clouds, and very cross, and then her spirits get so high that she's ready for any mischief—and there's no knowin' how to take her.'

'Isn't the wind dreadful, Jane?' said Clare presently. 'We couldn't have had a more dreary and depressing day for coming here.'

'It's terrible lonely, miss. How you young ladies will put up with it is more than Martha and me can imagine! My home is in the country, so I don't mind it. I never could abear London with its fog and dirt. Mrs. Tucker has been telling me and Martha queer tales about the gentleman who lived here.'

Clare wrapped herself in her dressing-gown and sat down by the fire. She rarely checked Jane's flow of talk, and perhaps that was why the maid liked her.

'What kind of tales?'

'Mrs. Tucker says he ought to have the property here called The Park, for he is the eldest son, and his younger brother, Major Lester, has taken it all, for Mr. Tom Lester offended his father by marrying a foreign lady, and he struck him out of his will. Mrs. Tucker says she believes the quarrel last autumn was about Major Lester's son, who is missing somewhere abroad, and who Mr. Tom Lester hates. And did you hear about the cupboard downstairs? Mrs. Tucker says she never has been inside it herself, for Mr. Lester only used to open it late at night, and he's gone away and taken the key with him, and says it isn't to be touched. I says to Mrs. Tucker that there might be anything in the cupboard, and Martha says she's afraid to go near it, for you do hear such dreadful tales about locked cupboards, and skeletons inside them, don't you, miss?'

'Only in your penny novelettes, that do you more harm than good, Jane!' said Clare a little shortly. I think if Mrs. Tucker is such a gossip, we shan't care to have her about the house. Where does she live now?'

'She's going to stay with her married sister in Brambleton, miss, and she's going out cooking if she can. I says to Martha that her tongue runned away with her, we could hardly get in a word, she talks so; but she's a very good-natured person, and has given Martha and me a lot of information about the neighbourhood.'

Clare did not respond, but soon dismissed Jane, and then sat for some time in dreams before her fire. At last with a little sigh she took hold of her Bible, to have her usual evening reading out of it. She turned to Nannie's Psalm, and listlessly scanned the verse that had been given her.

'Rest in the Lord, and wait patiently for Him.'

'Rest!' she mused; 'it is the one thing I never have really experienced. I always seem to be wishing for, and wanting, what never comes to me. I don't suppose any but a very old person who has lived her life, and has no hopes left, can rest and wait patiently. I don't know why I always seem waiting for something big to come and satisfy my life. I remember when first Hugh spoke to me, and we were engaged, I hoped I should be perfectly satisfied and happy, but in some ways he has disappointed me. He is so—so humdrum and easily pleased, and wrapped up in his profession. I wish he were more intellectual. I do love him, of course I do, but he hasn't filled my life as I thought he would. He doesn't understand some of my thoughts about things. I often wonder why I can't be as easily pleased with everybody and everything as Elfie is. Nannie would say it is because my religion is not real. I don't feel I could rest in the Lord. He seems far away, and there are so many difficulties, and sometimes I get to doubt everything! I wish I had Nannie's faith.'

She sighed again, and her thoughts came back to her present surroundings.

'I never shall like it here, I am sure; only it is no good to say so. It is such a depressing house, with not a sound outside, except this howling wind. I think it was a very doubtful venture coming down to a place where we know no one. Perhaps in the summer it will be better. I will try and not be discontented, but I feel to-night as if evil is coming upon us, and this awful wind seems to moan like a human being in the chimney. I think I will get into bed, and follow Gwen's advice. Oh dear, I wish I wasn't so easily depressed!'

But a sound night's rest made impressionable Clare view things rather differently the next day. The rain and wind had disappeared, and as she looked out of her window the first thing, she saw a cloudless blue sky, and the green meadows and pine woods in the distance, all lying in still bright sunshine. She opened her casement, and the fresh spring air fanned her cheeks, and brought her scents of the sweet country round her. She came downstairs to breakfast radiant; not even Elfie's sunny face could eclipse hers.

'It's delicious!' she exclaimed; 'I am longing to explore the garden. Is it as well stocked with fruit and vegetables as the advertisement led us to expect?'

'Yes, I think it is,' said Gwen; 'but of course everything has been very neglected. Mrs. Tucker assures me a nephew of hers always worked for Mr. Lester, and would be glad to come to us for the same wages. What do you think, Agatha? Can we afford eight shillings a week?'

Agatha looked a little worried.

'Oh, there is plenty of time to think of the garden later on. There is so much to do in the house. I hope you will all help in the unpacking to-day, or we shall never get straight.'

'Household cares already beginning!' said Elfie, laughing. 'Now I vote we all take a holiday this lovely day, and explore our surroundings; there's time enough to put the house straight later on.'

'Agatha will be miserable till every pin finds its place,' said

Amy Le Feuvre

Gwen. 'I promise that I'll work like a horse all this morning, but this afternoon I will have for pleasure.'

And this was how they finally settled it; and all four spent their morning in putting up curtains, hanging pictures, superintending the carpets and rugs being laid down, and sorting out and distributing the linen, plate, and china as it was needed.

Clare and Elfie sang as they worked, Gwen directed, scolded, and joked in turn, and Agatha was the only one who seemed to feel it a grave and solemn responsibility.

But they sat down to their luncheon with light hearts.

'We only want to fill the house with flowers to make it look really comfortable,' said Clare, 'and I mean to go and look for some this afternoon.'

Agatha could not be persuaded to leave the house. House-keeping was her forte, and she declared she would never sit down in comfort, till her store and linen cupboards were in perfect order.

The three others wandered first through the garden, and Gwen declared her intention of taking the whole of it under her superintendence.

'You don't know a thing about it,' said Elfie, saucily.

'Then I can learn. We are not going to live in the lap of luxury here, as you will soon discover. Our two maids will be rather different to our staff of servants in London.'

'Well, I tell you what I will do,' said Elfie: 'I'll help Martha with the cooking; I did a lot in Germany. I'll send you in the most delicious tea-cakes and biscuits for afternoon tea, and I'll teach her how to cook her vegetables after the German fashion!'

'Defend us from German grease, and odious mixtures of sweet and sour!' exclaimed Clare. 'Make us the tea-cakes, but leave the vegetables alone. Now take us down the village, Gwen, and let us see the church.'

They left the garden, and picked their way down the muddy lane until they reached the village street. Clare and Elfie were delighted with all they saw, especially with the old church. It had a typical country churchyard, with a large yew tree inside the old lych gate. The door was open, so they went in, and, though plain and rather bare in appearance, it possessed a beautiful stained window at the east end, several old tombs, and a handsome-looking organ. Elfie pressed forward eagerly to look at the latter, and found to her delight that it was open. Music was her passion, and she was almost as skilful at the organ as at her piano or with her violin.

'I must try it,' she whispered; 'do blow for me, one of you!'

Gwen complied with her request immediately, and strains of Mendelssohn and Handel were soon filling the church. Clare was wandering dreamily round listening and enjoying it, when suddenly a harsh voice behind her startled her.

'And may I ask who has given you permission to touch the organ?'

'I am not touching it,' Clare responded, coolly, gazing in astonishment at the apparition before her.

An old lady with a cap awry on her head, green spectacles, and a large shawl flung round her, stood tapping the ground impatiently with a walking-stick.

'I don't wish to meet with impertinence; your party are taking an unwarrantable liberty. I wish, if my brother persists in keeping the church doors open, that he would keep a chained bulldog inside! Nothing else will keep you tourists in your place. And here am I without a bonnet, defying St. Paul's command, and getting a fresh attack of rheumatism, and perhaps palpitation of the heart, by my haste and exposure! Will you have the goodness to tell your friends to leave that organ alone?'

Elfie, hearing voices, now turned round and left her seat at once.

Clare was not trying to soothe the old lady, but rather seemed to enjoy her irascibility.

'No, madam, we are not tourists. Are you the verger's wife? You must excuse my ignorance, but we are strangers in this part. Perhaps you can tell us a little about the church; it seems a very old one. How many years has it been standing?'

For answer the old lady raised her stick and tapped her slightly on the shoulder with it.

'Leave the church, young woman, and don't try to make me violent in the house of God!'

They were in the porch by this time, and Elfie and Gwen joined them. Elfie at once tried to make peace.

'I am very sorry,' she said contritely. 'I am so fond of the organ that I could not resist trying it. Please forgive me; I will not do it again unless I have permission.'

She smiled so sweetly as she spoke that the old lady seemed a little softened.

'You will never get my permission,' was all she said; and then she hobbled away like some malignant fairy, disappearing through a little wicket gate at the end of the churchyard, and making Gwen exclaim, 'She must be the clergyman's mother or aunt. Well, we have had a pleasant introduction! What will Agatha say?'

CHAPTER IV

BLUEBEARD'S CUPBOARD

'O most lame and impotent conclusion!'

—Shakespeare

Agatha was naturally very vexed when she heard from her sisters what had happened. She was sometimes laughed at by her friends for her devotion to the clergy, and all her hopes of doing good were centred in the country church and its organizations.

'It is most unfortunate,' she said; 'I was hoping that perhaps some of them might call before Sunday, but really after such an encounter they may totally ignore us. It was not right to do such a thing, Elfie, without permission. I can't think how Gwen could have allowed it.'

'Well, really, I am not up in propriety and etiquette in such matters,' was Gwen's rather impatient response. 'We are not in town now, thank goodness! In the country you are supposed to have a little freedom. If they don't wish people to try the organ, they should not leave it open, or they should chain a bulldog to the organ stool. Wasn't that her suggestion, Clare? My dear Agatha, don't fuss yourself. This old woman must be quite a character, and would abuse anybody, I feel certain. We didn't tell her who we were, so if she comes to call on you, we will keep out of the way. She seemed half blind, so I don't expect she would recognise us again.'

'Jane says she lives alone with her brother, who is un-married,' said Clare, 'and she is quite a Tartar in the village, though she is very good in relieving the villagers' wants.'

'What does Jane know about it?'

'Oh, she gets her gossip from Mrs. Tucker, who also told her that Miss Miller sees better through her green glasses than most people do without any glasses at all!'

'Mrs. Tucker talks a lot of rubbish, I expect,' said Gwen, rather loftily; then, changing the conversation, she said, 'I am going to unpack my books now. Who will come and help me? I am longing to fill up those empty bookshelves in Mr. Lester's study. What a good thing he left them as fixtures!'

'I will help you, if you like,' said Clare. 'Are you going to take sole possession of that study, may I ask?'

Gwen looked across at her rather queerly.

'Not if you dispute it,' she said, with a little laugh. 'Agatha is in love with the drawing-room. She has already arranged a corner for herself there; her writing-table in the west window, her work-basket and books in the corner by it, and her pet canary is now singing himself hoarse at the view he has from the window.'

'Yes,' Agatha replied, 'it is an ideal old maid's corner, and

Amy Le Feuvre

that is where you will always find me, when my house-keeping duties are not keeping me away.'

'I wish we could have a sitting-room each,' said Clare; 'we get so in each other's way.'

'You can share the study with me when you want to be quiet,' said Gwen. 'I won't have you there if you talk!'

'You're quite the owner of it already, then? And what are you going to do, Elfie?'

'Oh, I shall be everywhere. Agatha never minds my music. I shall be practising a good deal, and if I'm voted a bore, I shall take my violin up to the bedroom. You and Gwen are the blue stockings, so the study will be given over to you.'

This seemed satisfactory. Gwen was a great reader, and possessed already a most valuable library. She wrote essays for some periodical occasionally, but would never bind herself to any steady contributions, and she was never so happy as when deeply engrossed in some ancient histories of Egypt or Nineveh. The buried past had a fascination for her, and perhaps she of all the others had most reason for regretting the departure from London, for her constant visits to the reading-room at the British Museum had been a keen delight and pleasure to her. When quite a schoolgirl she used to say, with that masterful toss of her head, 'I am quite determined that I will understand and master every "ology" under the sun!'

And Gwen and her 'ologies' had been a perpetual joke in her family ever since. She had dabbled in a good many sciences —geology, astronomy, architecture, physiology, botany, natural history, and archaeology all had their turn, and she certainly seemed to get a good deal of interest and amusement out of them all. She announced to Clare, as a little later they were seated on the study floor surrounded by pyramids of books, that she intended to give her thoughts now to gardening and agriculture.

'I have some delightful old books on horticulture, which I shall read up,' she said enthusiastically; 'and there is an old Dutch writer amongst them who gives the most minute directions for laying out a flower and vegetable garden. I have told Agatha I shall take the garden into my charge. I am certain I shall succeed with it.'

'Do you ever doubt your capability for doing anything?'

Clare put the question gravely.

'No, I don't think I do, except teach a Sunday school class!' said Gwen, laughing.

'I sometimes feel I am incapable of living even,' said Clare dreamily.

Gwen stared at her. These two understood each other better than one would have thought possible with such opposite characteristics. Clare admired Gwen's intellect, and there were times when Gwen knew that Clare had depths of which she knew nothing. Reason and practical common sense had full sway in the one, imagination and mysticism in the other, and none of these qualities were tempered with real religion.

'You must be in the blues!' exclaimed Gwen, with a laugh.

'No,' said Clare, looking up, 'I am not, at all. I am longing to be up and doing, and leave some mark behind me as I go. Is that Browning you have in your hand? Just let me look up a passage!' Gwen laughed again as she handed across the book.

'No hope for any more help from you, if you once get hold of him!'

And for an hour Clare sat amongst the piles of books with her fair head resting against the carved cupboard, and not a word or sign could Gwen get out of her.

Elfie spent her time in helping Agatha to unpack, and it was a very tired little party that gathered round the drawing-room fire that evening.

'I wonder,' said Clare, 'if we shall find we have made a mistake in coming here. It seems so very quiet, and different to either London or Dane Hall. When we used to stay there with Aunt Mildred, there was always such a lot going on that it didn't seem quite like the country.'

'My dear Clare,' said Agatha quietly, 'you would be much happier yourself, and would make others happier too, if you always made the best of your circumstances. I remember you used to complain at Dane Hall of the frivolity and empty-headedness of aunt's visitors, and would say it was a mere waste of life to live as we did!'

'Oh, don't be so prosy, Agatha!' Clare returned impatiently. 'If you were dropped into a workhouse ward, you would look round and remark how comfortable you were, and how at last you had found your vocation!'

Elfie laughed aloud at this, but Agatha leant back in her chair and looked into the glowing coals in front of her with a smile that showed she was not destitute of humour. 'I daresay I might,' she said. 'I always love a community of old women, and if I could have chats with them, I am sure I should enjoy myself.'

'Well, I only wish I could be so easily contented,' said Clare, in a tone that showed she would be very sorry for herself if she were. She soon went off to bed, and Elfie followed, and then the two elder ones drew their chairs together and had a confidential talk over ways and means.

Agatha, though apparently apathetic at times and of a yielding disposition, had not always been so. When she first came home from school, she had all the bright hopes and restless longings of a young girl, and her aunt did all in her power to make life pleasant and bright for her. She went out into society, and was a general favourite, owing to her sweet temper and extreme unselfishness. Then one came on the scene who attracted her heart from the first. He was an earnest, whole-hearted Christian man, a vicar of an East End parish, and it was his influence that made Agatha view life in a different light. She vexed her aunt at first by gradually withdrawing from gaieties, and it was only with great difficulty that she was given permission to visit in the slums. The vicar was soon her betrothed, and Agatha had a few months of perpetual sunshine. But hard work, and a not very strong constitution, soon brought about a serious break-down, and he was ordered to the south of France to recruit his health. The parting was a sad one, and Agatha had wild thoughts of marrying then and there, and going with him as his wife and nurse. But this Miss Dane strenuously opposed, and poor Agatha had to bear the strain of five months away from the one who needed her so badly. He died, and for a time she was broken-hearted; but gradually she came to prove the reality and comfort of her religion, and then, taking up the interests of those around her, she had cheerfully buried her own sorrow, and became the mainstay of her aunt and her household. Perhaps Agatha felt most keenly being shut out from her aunt's dying room, she certainly uttered with heartfelt fervour morning and evening, 'Forgive us our trespasses, as we forgive those that trespass against us.'

And she had never trusted herself to mention her cousin's unjust dealing to anyone; even her sisters had little idea how deep her feelings were about it.

The next few days were very busy ones. Saturday brought Captain Knox, to stay with them till Monday, and Clare showed him over house and garden in the best of spirits. 'It is rather strange,' he said, as he sat at dinner with them that night, 'but one of my sisters knows a lady in this neighborhood, and she thinks you will like her. She lives somewhere on the outskirts of Brambleton. A Miss Villars. She is a charming woman, I hear, very comfortably off, but rather eccentric in the way she spends her money. My sister wrote to her when she knew of your arrival here, so you may have a visit from her soon.'

'Is she an old maid?' asked Elfie; 'because we have seen one, and, I was going to say, don't want to see another.'

Clare related their adventure in the church, and Captain Knox was much amused.

'I do not think there is anything queer about Miss Villars, except that she is a very religious woman.'

'Is that queer?' questioned Clare, a little wistfully.

'No,' Agatha said very quietly; 'it ought not to be.'

'But it is in the sight of the world,' retorted Captain Knox; 'that is, if your religion in an aggressive one.'

'Well, of course it ought not to be aggressive,' said Gwen briskly. 'Religion is a matter to be lived, not talked about. It only concerns oneself, and no one else.'

'That is a very selfish creed,' said Agatha. 'If you possess something good, you ought to wish to pass it on.'

'But not to thrust it on people who don't want it. I am thirsty, and like a glass of water, but need I insist upon your drinking it, when you are not thirsty at all?'

'Gwen loves an argument,' said Captain Knox good-naturedly.

'I am not good at arguing,' said Agatha, 'only, knowing that thirst can be a blessing, I think we should try to make people thirsty.'

'How do you mean?' asked Clare with interest, 'thirst is not, generally, a very happy experience.'

'Doesn't it say, "Blessed are they who hunger and thirst after righteousness, for they shall be filled"?'

'Oh, come, Agatha, we don't want a sermon with our dinner. You are not given to preach, so don't be trying to show us that you know how to be aggressive.'

Gwen's tone was a little scornful, and Agatha said no more; but as Clare was pacing up and down in the verandah with Captain Knox, a little time after, she suddenly said, 'I think I am a thirsty person, Hugh, only I never can tell what it is I am thirsting for; tell me, are you perfectly satisfied with yourself and with life?'

Captain Knox looked down at the sweet, pensive face of his betrothed. 'I shall be, Clare—on our wedding day.'

Clare frowned. 'You never will be in earnest about anything; you always turn my thoughts into ridicule.'

'Indeed I do not. But I am a plain, matter-of-fact soldier, and live on earth; you are in dreamland half your time, or in the clouds. Clare, darling, I cannot bear the thoughts of Africa sometimes; how shall I be able to stand being away from you so long? And time is slipping away so fast; only a fortnight more before I am off.'

'You will come down again before you start, of course?'

'Oh yes, I certainly intend to do so; but I have a lot to do in town—it may be only the last day that you will see me.'

Clare sighed, but said nothing, and then Captain Knox said suddenly,—

'Is Agatha very religious, Clare?

'No, I don't think so—not particularly. She is fond of church and all that, but she doesn't often speak out as she did at dinner to-night. Now, don't let us be gloomy; come indoors, and I will show you Bluebeard's cupboard in the study, It is well worth looking at, for it is beautifully carved, and I am going to try and copy it. You know how I love carving.'

She took him to the study, and there, by the aid of a lamp, they examined the old oak cupboard in the deep recess at the side of the fireplace.

'The strange thing is that there seems to be no lock or opening at all to it,' said Clare. 'I have spent hours in trying to find out where it is opened. Do you think one day I shall touch a spring, the doors will fly open, and there we shall see his headless wives?'

She was laughing now, and full of animation. Captain Knox passed his fingers lightly across the carving.

'I expect one of these carved bits is movable,' he said. 'It is a handsome bit of handicraft. What is this along the bottom, a scroll with writing?'

'That is what I say it is; Gwen says not, but I am sure those hieroglyphics mean something.'

It looks like Arabic characters,' said Captain Knox with interest. 'I believe it is so. Here, stop a minute; let me copy these in my notebook. I shall be studying Arabic on my way out, and if I find I can translate this, I will let you know.'

'Perhaps it is a clue to the mystery,' said Clare, with shining eyes; 'I am dying to know what this cupboard contains. Mrs. Tucker said she never saw it opened the whole time she was here; but Mr. Lester told her once that he prized this cupboard more than anything else in the house. She thinks, foolish woman, that it is full of gold! I only hope she won't spread that notion about Brambleton. The next thing will be that we shall have thieves in the house, and perhaps be all murdered in our beds!' Captain Knox laughed at her fears, and soon after, they joined the others in the drawing-room.

Amy Le Feuvre

CHAPTER V

A QUIET SUNDAY

'O day most calm, most bright,
The fruit of this, the next world's bud.

    *   *   *   *

The week were dark, but for thy light,
Thy torch doth show the way.'

—G. Herbert

The sisters, accompanied by Captain Knox, made quite a sensation in the little village church when they entered it on that Sunday morning. The old sexton fussed about as if all the seats were occupied; but eventually they were shown into one just beside the pulpit stairs. Miss Miller glared at them through her green spectacles, and Elfie felt miserably conscious that she had recognised them. There were a few other gentle-people in the church besides themselves, and a very fair sprinkling of farmers and villagers. The service was simple and hearty; the village schoolmaster played the organ, and Mr. Miller, a fine-looking, grey-headed man, delighted Agatha at least, by his earnest, faithful preaching. Coming out into the churchyard, Agatha was stopped by Miss Miller hastening up to her. She was dressed in black silk; but her bonnet, a wonderful erection of lace and ribbon, was quite awry, and she seemed agitated. She spoke jerkily, and Agatha had difficulty in preserving her usual equanimity of mind.

'Excuse me, but I believe you have taken Mr. Tom Lester's house—a most unsatisfactory parishioner he is, and not at all what he should be. I am hoping to call on you this week. Who is the gentleman? your brother? No? A great pity, then, for a houseful of women is only a hot-bed for scandal and gossip. We have too many women by far in this neighbourhood—a bachelor parson always draws them. Have you any acquaintances in the neighbourhood? Ah, so much the better. There is service at half-past six this evening; I hope you will be regular attendants. You live in a godless house; take care that the atmosphere does not affect you. Mr. Tom Lester never entered the House of God after I spoke to him about the irreverence of his yawns during the sermon! Goodbye, and I hope you will prove pleasant neighbours. That remains to be seen!'

She darted away as quickly as she came; and Elfie, who was walking with Agatha, gave one of her merry, rippling laughs.

'Isn't she an odd character? We shall have a good deal of fun out of her, I am sure! I am thankful she did not recognise me, or at least had the good taste not to appear as if she did.'

'I wonder,' said Agatha thoughtfully, 'if that old man who sat behind Miss Miller was our landlord's brother.'

'Oh, he was much too nice-looking; I imagine the other Mr. Lester is an awful old curmudgeon. He has got his property unjustly, I consider—the eldest son ought to have it.'

'Cousin James is not an old curmudgeon,' put in Gwen, stepping back to join in the conversation; 'supplanters and usurpers generally carry all the world before them, "like green bay trees," as the Psalmist says. I am sure our Jacob is most prepossessing in manner and appearance, like his namesake. History repeats itself!'

'Don't be bitter after church,' said Agatha, in her quiet voice.

Gwen laughed. 'I'm not bitter. I feel I can snap my fingers at him now! Hugh says he saw him in town the other day, and he said with his pleasant smile, "When we are quite settled at Dane Hall my wife will ask the girls down. They will be glad of the change, I expect, after their seclusion in the country!" Wasn't it truly kind and considerate of him?'

That first Sunday in the country was a very pleasant one to the sisters, Clare went off for a long walk with Hugh in the afternoon; Agatha settled herself in a wicker chair with her books in the sunny verandah overlooking the meadows and distant pine woods; and Gwen and Elfie wandered off across the fields, enjoying the sweet spring air, and noting all the spring flowers peeping out of the hedgerows.

'Yes, I'm thankful we are out of town,' said Gwen emphatically, standing up and drawing in long breaths of content and satisfaction. 'If I were starving, I would rather be in the country, because one can be clean. It's the oppression in the atmosphere that is so sickening in London, and never being able to get away from people!'

'This is an ideal Sunday,' said Elfie, turning her radiant face upwards and watching a lark soaring out of sight; 'I don't think I shall miss the concerts in town, with such music as this around one!'

Then after a pause she said, 'I suppose becoming lazy and self-indulgent is a danger in the country.'

'We are not rich enough for that,' responded Gwen with a short laugh; 'at least, I know I have my work cut out for me.'

'I wasn't meaning actual daily duties, but our responsibilities regarding others,' said Elfie, a little shyly.

Gwen shrugged her shoulders. 'I suppose you feel you ought to be in Sunday school this afternoon, is that it? I dare say Miss Miller will give you some parish work, if you ask her. Are you going to follow in Agatha's steps? I saw her from my bedroom window this morning stop a carter going by from the farm, and hand him some tracts.'

Elfie laughed. 'She's a good old thing; she never says anything about her good deeds, but I know she will soon be fast friends with all the farm labourers who pass up and down. You see if next week she doesn't know all their names and family histories!'

They were crossing a fresh meadow now, and as they came up to a stile, they saw in the next field a most picturesque little cottage standing in the midst of a mass of apple blossom. It was a low white-washed building, with thatched roof and latticed windows, green shutters opening back upon the wall.

The girls went up, and leaning against the gate, looked at it admiringly; then started at the sight of two oldish women sitting opposite one another in the old-fashioned porch. They were dressed exactly alike, two lilac sun-bonnets hiding their faces; their figures were thin and angular, and each had a book in her lap. Their dark-blue serge gowns, white aprons, and little red worsted shawls over their shoulders, were

Amy Le Feuvre

duplicates one of the other.

'It's like a book,' whispered Elfie. 'Do let us speak to them. We can ask them where the footpath leads to!'

Gwen opened the gate, and accordingly put the question.

Both women started to their feet, and one came forward.

'Where does this footpath lead to? Why, to our cottage, and no further, miss.'

She spoke respectfully, though rather shortly.

'I am afraid we have trespassed,' said Elfie, in her sweet, bright tone; 'but we are strangers here, and are trying to find our way about. What a lovely little cottage you have!'

'It's a tidy little place,' the woman responded, with an approving nod. 'Perhaps you'd like to come in and sit for a bit. Patty and me don't care for Sunday visitin', but you'll be the ladies from Jasmine Cottage, I reckon?'

'Yes,' said Gwen, 'we will come in for a minute before we go back.'

They followed her into a spotlessly clean and tidy kitchen. Patty drew forward two chairs, and began to speak rather breathlessly. 'My sister and me saw you in church to-day. We said you were the new family; and Deb is very good at upholsterin' and alterin' carpets, and doin' plain needlework, and we thought maybe you'd be wantin' help that way, for Deb goes to work by the day at most of the big houses round!'

'Tis the Lord's Day,' said Deb, giving her sister a sharp nudge with her elbow; 'we'll not be talking business now. Sit down, ladies.'

Gwen and Elfie exchanged amused glances. Then Gwen said,—

'Well, we won't transact business now; but we want a workwoman badly, and if you will come to the cottage tomorrow my sister will show you any amount of carpets that need refitting. But if I had a cottage like this, away from all sound and sight of any human beings, I think I wouldn't trouble to go out carpet-making!'

'You would if you wanted to keep your cottage,' said Deb brusquely. Then, taking off her sun-bonnet and smoothing down her grey hair, she sat down on an old oak settle beside the little cheery blazing fire, and grasping her angular knees with each hand, she looked at Given a little defiantly.

'Eight and forty year come next Christmas have Patty and I lived together here, and never a year have we been behind our rent since father died; but it have been done by downright hard labour. And if you and your people want new-laid eggs, or fresh spring chickens, or honey from the comb, why, 'tis Patty that will supply you, as also milk and butter from an Alderney cow.'

"Tis Sunday!' ejaculated Patty, as she stood by the fire with arms akimbo; and at this retort Gwen and Elfie laughed outright.

'And do you ever go away from home?' asked Gwen curiously, after a slight pause, in which Deb looked very discomposed.

'We are continually away,' said Deb, looking up and

speaking very shortly. 'I know every gentry's house in the neighbourhood, not to speak of Brambleton, where Patty goes reg'lar once a week to market. But as to sleepin' away, that we never mean to do till we be taken to our last restin'-place!'

'And are you great readers? I am afraid we disturbed you from your books when we came in.'

Patty took up her book, which was on the window-ledge. ''Tis Bunyan's book, *The Pilgrim's Progress*. Father give Deb and me a copy each when we were fifteen years old, and we have read it every Sunday afternoon since. We don't always get very far, for 'tis a sleepy time in the afternoon, but a page or two is always edifyin' and improvin' to the soul!'

'It's a lovely book!' said Elfie enthusiastically; 'you must know it nearly by heart.'

The sisters smiled at each other.

'We do that,' said Deb.

'I suppose you have visitors from the village here occasionally?' asked Gwen.

Deb frowned grimly, then looked her questioner straight in the face, with hard-set lines about her mouth, as she replied,—

'We keeps ourselves to ourselves, miss. You are both young ladies, and haven't lived long enough to have it cast up in your teeth that you're not wed; but there be those who scorn us for choosin' to keep by each other, and not do as most young maids do. Patty and me have had our chances, but Patty's lad couldn't take us both, and 'twas the same with my lad, and neither of us could bear to be away from the other.

We've always grown together, Patty and me—we came into the world together, and we pray the Lord He'll take us out in the same manner; and we know each other's ways, and when we don't agree, there's no one else to interfere.'

'Do you ever disagree?' asked Elfie, smiling.

Patty nodded her head solemnly.

'Ay, we ain't quite the same make through and through,' she said, in her little breathless way, 'and words run high at times. I keep to my opinions, and Deb keeps to hers; and if we have an extra hard dispute on, we know how to settle it!'

'How? with fists?' asked Gwen, looking from one hard-featured woman to the other with the greatest interest.

Deb looked up grimly, and said, as she raised her hand in emphasis,—

'Patty have never had a blow from me since we were children, nor I from her. When our tongues run away with us, one locks the t'other out, and when we get cool again the door is opened!'

'I would rather be inside than outside on a winter's day,' said Gwen, laughing heartily. 'Now come, Elfie, we must be off. I shall pay you another visit before long, to learn about bee-keeping. I see your hives are just like ours, and we know nothing about such things!'

'And I'll be very glad to tell you,' said Patty eagerly, 'for I've tended bees since I were a child, and know all their tricks, and as to their swarmings.'

"Tis the Lord's Day,' put in Deb grimly, and Gwen and Elfie

Amy Le Feuvre

promptly took their leave.

'Aren't they old dears?' said Elfie enthusiastically; 'they seem to live in quite another world. Imagine reading *The Pilgrim's Progress* all your life, and no other book beside the Bible! Do they ever see a newspaper, I wonder?'

'It isn't often one meets such a couple; we shall get a good deal of entertainment out of them, I expect. What an awful existence! Is it what we shall come to years hence, I wonder? And yet I, for one, am quite certain that will not be my lot.'

'What?' inquired Elfie, 'the old maid's existence, do you mean, or the little secluded country cottage?'

'Neither. I have my plans and purposes; and not all Jacob's machinations and schemings will frustrate them.'

'What are they?' inquired Elfie.

'Ah, well, I had best not say. I mean to see you all thoroughly comfortable and settled here, and then break them to you. I have plenty of resources and interests to take up my time, so am in no hurry.'

'You always were a wonderful one for plans! Let me guess. You are going to start a magazine, and be the editor of it!'

'No, thank you. Magazines are as plentiful as pins just now; they appear and disappear like sky-rockets!'

'Is it a way of earning money?'

'No, of spending it; but I am not going to tell you. I generally find I can carry out my plans successfully, if I don't take too many people into my confidence!'

Elfie was silent for a few minutes; then she said, with a little sigh, 'I wonder how old Nannie is getting on?'

'What has put her into your head?'

'The verses she gave us. Don't you remember?'

'I'm sure I forget what mine was.'

"'Commit thy way unto the Lord, trust also in Him, and He shall bring it to pass,'" said Elfie softly.

'Nannie never could stand my independence. I believe she thought we ought not to have taken this cottage without first having prayer about it!'

'Agatha did pray about it,' said Elfie very quietly.

'Well, I didn't, and I was the one to find it, and it has turned out quite a success. I never can understand such narrow views of life as Agatha takes. Prayer is all very well in church, or in great crises, but in everyday life I think it is perfectly unnatural and unnecessary!'

Elfie did not answer. She felt too inexperienced to argue the matter out with Gwen, though she totally disagreed with her.

They reached home, and found Clare and Captain Knox before them. Afternoon tea was had in the drawing-room, and afterwards, before evening church, Elfie brought her violin out, and Agatha went to the piano, whilst the others gathered round and sang some hymns with them. The evening closed quietly and peacefully; and as Captain Knox said good-night to his betrothed, he added, 'I am so glad I have seen you all here. I shall picture your quiet Sundays when I am in the wilds of Africa, and it will do me good!'

Amy Le Feuvre

CHAPTER VI

A DEPARTURE

'The heart which like a staff was one
For mine to lean and rest upon,
The strongest on the longest day,
With steadfast love, is caught away,
And yet my days go on, go on.'

—E. B. Browning

Miss Miller came to call with her brother a few days after-wards. Agatha and Elfie were busy putting some finishing touches to the drawing-room when they arrived.

Miss Miller looked round the room, when she was seated, with some interest; and then she said abruptly,—

'Too much furniture, and too many useless ornaments, my dears. A drawing-room ought to be for use, and not for show. Who arranges your flowers?'

She might well ask, for none but an artist's hand could have grouped together so harmoniously the daffodils and primroses, with trails of ivy and fern in their beds of moss.

'Clare does,' responded Elfie brightly, sitting down by her side, whilst Agatha turned to the vicar. 'She went out this morning and picked them in a wood close to us. Aren't they lovely?'

'Not Major Lester's wood, I hope. He will not be best pleased to have any one from this house trespassing in his places. Miss Dane, do you know the history of your house?'

Agatha looked up, a little startled at the sharp voice. 'I did not know it had any history,' she said.

'It is best you should know facts. No, Wilfrid, you need not stop me; they will hear our village gossip fast enough. To begin with—your house used to be the old vicarage. It was built on the site of an old monastery. Our church is four hundred years old. The monastery came to grief long before the church. When old Squire Lester died, most of us thought the Hall would go to Mr. Tom. He had always been erratic and restless, spending most of his time abroad, and the squire never forgave his marriage with a French artist's daughter. He disinherited him, and made his second son leave the army and come home. A couple of years after, Mr. Tom returned, having lost his wife, and bringing a little son with him, a boy of four years. The old squire seemed to relent a little then, and was always having the child at the house. Mr. Tom, as we call him here, settled in this house, and was on friendly terms with his father till his death. Major Lester then took the property. He had an only son, too; and the boys, being of the same age, were much together; but their fathers would hardly speak to each other, and were angry at the friendship between the boys. I remember being at Major Lester's the very day of the sad event. I was calling on Mrs. Lester, and we heard a violent altercation going on in the hall between the brothers. Mr. Tom had come up for his son, who had made him anxious by his non-appearance at home the night

Amy Le Feuvre

before. The lads had been out for a night's rabbit-snaring with the gamekeeper, and Alick had slept at the Hall without the major's knowledge. I don't know why this should have led to such a violent quarrel, but Alick was summoned from the stables, where he was found with his cousin Roger, and forbidden ever to put his foot on Major Lester's property again. Then and there the lads were separated; but as Mr. Tom marched off with his son, he shouted out to his brother, "You'll live to see my son stand in Roger's shoes yet, and the property will come back to the rightful heir!"

'I remember Mrs. Lester turning to me, and trembling like a leaf: "He will murder Roger! The dreadful man!" she exclaimed; "that is the only way the property will come to Alick!"

'The very next day both boys were missing. Mr. Tom seemed quite as distracted as his brother, but he declared he knew nothing of them, and for a month no tidings were received, in spite of all the detectives at work. Then came a letter from Alick, written for both of them, saying they had taken their passage together for Australia, and had already got the promise of being taken on a farm; for they were made so miserable at home by the quarrels of their fathers, that they had "determined to clear out of it," and nothing would separate them from each other. They have not been in this neighbourhood since; but last autumn news came that Roger had disappeared. Alick wrote, giving details:—"I think Roger was sent on some confidential errand by the farmer, for he had money with him, and they fear that he was robbed, perhaps murdered on the way." Mrs. Lester, who was never very strong, took to her bed, and died a fortnight after the news was brought to her. But before she died she emphatically declared that Mr. Tom and his son had decoyed Roger out of the country to make away with him; and Alick was solely responsible for his death. She persisted in this until the major more than half believed it; and two days after the funeral he came down here, and had another most violent quarrel with his brother. It almost came to blows; and Mr. Tom decamped altogether within a week from that time. I only tell you the story. Some people here think badly of him, and his disappearance looks suspicious. Of course he gave out that he was going to Australia to find out the rights of it; but Major Lester does not believe this.'

'I wonder Major Lester does not go out himself,' said Agatha, feeling strangely interested in this story.

'He is too crippled by gout to do so. He has put the matter into the hands of the police out there. It's a sad story. The major is most regular at church, and highly respected in the neighbourhood. Mr. Tom is most erratic; I believe he has been seen in the Methodist chapel occasionally, but won't put his foot inside our church; and he is no loss at all to the neighbourhood, for he lived the life of a recluse. I always look upon this house as an ill-omened place. I didn't tell you that the last vicar who lived here died of delirium tremens. He was a disgrace to his profession, but that was thirty years ago. The new vicarage was built shortly after.' Miss Miller paused for breath, and her brother remarked, 'You must not prejudice the Miss Danes, Deborah, against their house. It is a quaint place, and its past need not be recorded.'

'We are charmed with it,' said Agatha simply; 'and we have moved into it at the right time. Spring in the country is always so delightful.'

Miss Miller was more agreeable when visiting than Agatha had hoped for, and though she insisted on the monopoly of the conversation, and gave the good vicar little chance of putting in a word, yet Agatha felt that they would be pleasant neighbours. There was a good deal of discussion over the

Amy Le Feuvre

Lesters' history, but Gwen dismissed the subject in her usual way.

'Major Lester is another Jacob. There's nothing more to be said, and Mr. Tom is a much-abused and misunderstood man!'

Agatha began to settle into her new life very happily. She became engrossed in housekeeping for several hours every morning, and was delighted to hear of a seamstress who could come in and work by the day. Deb Howitt was sent for, and she proved a skilful and industrious needlewoman, and amused and interested all who came in contact with her by her quaint remarks.

'Yes,' she remarked to Gwen, who had strolled into Agatha's bedroom one morning, and found Deb seated on the floor shaping a refractory carpet that would not fit, 'my sister is the stay-at-home, and I bring her the news of the world as I pick it up when I'm out visitin'. It's surprisin' the stories of high and low life that I hear. I take it all in, and think it over while I'm stitchin', and come to many a wise conclusion before I take it back with me and talk it over with Patty.'

'And what conclusion will you come to about us?' asked Gwen.

The old woman nodded her head with a meaning smile.

'Ay, well, ye're a house full of women, and there's an astonishin' little scoldin' and quarrellin'. I should say, taking the cluster of you together, that the one at either end keeps the peace in the middle.'

Gwen laughed delightedly. 'You are right: Agatha and Elfie are the peace-makers, Clare and I the disturbing elements!

What else?'

But Deb shook her head, and would say no more.

Clare and Gwen shared the study very amicably together, but both were out of doors a great deal—Gwen tackling the untidy garden with a great deal of energy, but little experience; and Clare wandering about the lanes and fields, doing little, and dreaming much. Then came Captain Knox's farewell visit, and it was a very short one. He appeared at seven o'clock one evening, just as the sisters were sitting down to their high tea, which meal they had substituted for the orthodox dinner to which they had been accustomed in London.

Clare's cheeks grew pale as she greeted him. 'How long have you?' she asked, a little breathlessly.

'Till eight o'clock to-morrow morning. I must catch the 8.30 train from Brambleton. We sail to-morrow afternoon.'

It was rather a silent meal, and being a rough, stormy night Clare took him off to the study directly afterwards. She was in the mood that pleased her lover best: sweet and gentle, and showing more affection than she was wont to do, for she was not demonstrative usually.

'Hugh,' she said later in the evening, after sitting still and letting him do most of the talking, 'I wish I were going with you. I feel as if this parting is going to be a long one. I can't bear this wind and rain to-night—it makes me feel as if something awful is coming; it was just the same the first night we were here. I have a kind of presentiment about your going, as if something evil is coming upon us. Couldn't you give it up?'

Captain Knox smiled a little, though his face looked troubled as he drew her closer to him.

'My darling, you would not really wish me to. We must look forward to six months hence, when I return, and then, Clare, I shall wait no longer. You must come to me for good and all.'

Clare did not reply for a minute, then gently slipping her hand into the strong one near her, she said, very wistfully, 'Hugh, don't you think we should both have more comfort if we had more religion? I haven't enough of it to satisfy me, I think. Now Agatha trusts everything in her life to—to God, and is never worried or anxious. I can't do that, and oh, I'm so unsatisfied! You don't know how restless and wretched I feel sometimes! I should like to be able to pray for you properly when you are away, and feel that you were praying for me.'

Captain Knox was silent for a little, then he said quietly,—

'I have a certain amount of religion, as you know, and you couldn't have too much for me, at least as long as you keep it to yourself. I think every woman is the better for being truly religious; but we men who knock about amongst all kinds of evil, well, we can't expect to be very devout. It is soon knocked out of one. Pray for me as much as you like, darling; I need it!'

'I can't help thinking of Nannie's verse she gave me one evening,' said Clare, with a little sigh: '"Rest in the Lord, and wait patiently for Him." It sounds so nice; but I don't know how to do it. And I am sure I shall need patience till you come back again!'

'We must write to each other, and think of next autumn. I shall not forget to send you the translation of those characters on that old cupboard. I am convinced they are Arabic.'

'Oh, bother the cupboard!' was Clare's petulant retort. 'It is too bad you are going away for so long, and you take it so coolly. I don't believe you mind a bit!'

Here she burst into a passion of tears, and poor Captain Knox, who was controlling his feelings for her sake, almost gave way himself.

It was not a happy evening, and Clare cried herself to sleep that night, feeling that she was the most unfortunate, wretched girl in the world. She crept down the next morning with a white face to give him his early breakfast, and then drove to Brambleton station with him; so no one saw the last parting. When she returned, she went upstairs to her room, and shut herself up for the rest of the morning.

'It is a pity Clare did not show her affection for him more when she was with him,' said Gwen impatiently, when Agatha came to her in the study, and wondered if she should go up and try to comfort her. 'I often marvel at Hugh's infatuation for her. I don't believe she knows what real love is. She is so taken up with her own feelings and moods, that she has no time for his, and I think he is far too good for her. If she is so discontented before marriage, what will she be afterwards? He will have a miserable time of it, I am afraid!'

'You are too hard upon her! I daresay his absence will prove to her how truly she loves him, for I am quite sure she does.'

'I have no patience with her!' said Gwen shortly; and then she buried herself in her book again, whilst Agatha went away and shed some tears herself over Captain Knox's departure.

CHAPTER VII

UNREST

'Thou hast made us for Thyself,
And our hearts are restless
till they rest in Thee.

—St. Augustine

Some weeks passed. The girls were perfectly satisfied with their quiet country life. Elfie brightened the whole house with her music and high spirits. Agatha soon found her way to the nearest cottages, and was friends with all the farm labourers who passed by the house, and Gwen tried to manage everything and everybody. Clare shook off her low spirits, but was uncertain-tempered, and would never settle at any occupation for long at a time. Still, she delighted in the country round, and would return from her rambles with her arms full of Nature's treasures, making the little house beautiful with her lovely flowers and greenery.

Miss Miller fussed in and out, and was very glad of Agatha's help in parish matters; even unbending so far as to give Elfie permission to play on the organ in church, which, of course, delighted her. Agatha was informed that she could visit as freely as she liked, but that no relief was to be given, except through the vicarage.

'I look after everybody myself. I know the deserving and the undeserving, and they know me! I won't have anything given to my parishioners without my knowledge. My brother leaves it all in my hands.'

One afternoon Miss Villars called, and found only Clare at home. She was a sweet-looking, attractive woman, and Clare, with her usual impulsiveness, lost her heart to her at once. She confided to her the history of her engagement, and parting with Captain Knox; and the visit lengthened into nearly an hour before Miss Villars took her leave.

Clare went into raptures about her, when talking to her sisters afterwards.

'She is not a bit goody or eccentric, as Hugh hinted. She talked and laughed as naturally as any one; and she has such a lovely face. Dresses very quietly, but with good taste; and is such a graceful woman! She is quite the nicest person I have met for a long time. I am dying to see her in her own home. I am sure it must be a charming one. She drove over in an open carriage with a handsome pair of horses; and has offered to take us for drives whenever we like.'

'We really must afford ourselves a small trap,' said Gwen. 'We cannot do without it in the country. If we had a donkey, it would be better than nothing!'

'*I* wouldn't go in a donkey-cart,' said Clare, with disdain.

'Then you could stay at home. Agatha, what do you say? We have a stable. How much will it cost, do you think?'

When once Gwen took a matter in hand, she generally carried it through; and very shortly after, the sisters were the proud possessors of a little two-wheeled trap, and a small rough pony. This was a great convenience as well as pleasure to them, and when Clare had a fit of the blues, she would go off to Brambleton and do some shopping, and return quite interested and eager to tell all she had seen and heard. She met Miss Villars on one of her expeditions, and she asked her to go and have a cup of tea with her before she returned home. This Clare willingly did. She had not been to the house before, though Agatha and Gwen had; but she found it quite answered her expectations. It was an ideal old-fashioned country house, and Miss Villars was a perfect hostess. She introduced Clare to a delicate-looking girl staying with her: 'This is Miss Audrey Foster, who enjoys the country quite as much as you do.'

'It is paradise to me,' said the girl enthusiastically. 'I am a Londoner, and have never stayed in the country before.'

Clare looked at her, and noted that her shabby serge dress and pale pinched face seemed strangely incongruous with her surroundings. But when she had left the room shortly afterwards, Miss Villars said: 'Miss Foster is the eldest daughter of an East End vicar. She has not had a holiday or any change from home since her school-days; and she is mother and governess to five younger brothers and sisters. I hope to send her back a different creature. It is a great pleasure to give pleasure to other people, is it not?'

'I don't think I ever have,' said Clare frankly.

'Ah, well, my circumstances have made it easy for me to do so. My house is too big to live alone in it, and so I have relays of young visitors who need a little brightness in their lives. It is so sad to think of some young lives being cramped and dwarfed by their surroundings; and some natures utterly sink beneath the burden of household cares and anxieties, that ought not to touch them at all in youth.'

'You are very good, Miss Villars, are you not?'

Miss Villars laughed brightly. 'Not at all, my dear child. I wish I were.'

'I wish I were too,' said Clare, with sudden impulse. 'You look so happy—I wish I knew your secret.'

'"Happy is that people whose God is the Lord,"' said Miss Villars softly.

Clare sighed. 'I never have found religion make me happy, Miss Villars.'

'No more have I. It is only the Lord Himself who can do that. Do you know Him as your Friend and Saviour?'

Clare had never had such a question put to her before. 'I don't know Him at all,' she said earnestly; 'God seems such a long way off.'

'You know how you can get near Him?'

'By being very religious, I suppose.'

'The Bible doesn't say so. It says this: "But now in Christ Jesus ye who sometimes were far off are made nigh by the blood of Christ. For He is our peace, who hath made both one, and hath broken down the middle wall of partition between us." Think that verse over, dear, and look it up in your own Bible.'

Amy Le Feuvre

'But,' said Clare, hesitating a little, 'I don't think I want to be brought nearer to God. That has no attraction for me.'

'Then you will never know real happiness. Any soul away from its Creator knows no peace.'

Clare was silent, and then Miss Foster entered the room again, and the subject was changed; but Clare had plenty of food for reflection as she drove home.

It was a lovely afternoon in June—so warm that for once the four sisters were together in the shady verandah outside the drawing-room windows, taking their ease and waiting for their afternoon tea. Agatha was the only one who was doing anything, and she was stitching away at some small garment for one of the farm carter's children. It was a still, drowsy afternoon; the very bees seemed too lazy to hum, and were settling sleepily on the rose bushes close to their hives.

'This is the most sleepy time in the day,' observed Gwen, leaning back in her low wicker chair, her head resting on her arms behind it, 'I could go to sleep in five minutes if I chose; there is not a creature moving for miles round us, I expect.'

'I love the stillness,' said Clare. 'Every one in the country has time to rest. How different it is in London!'

'I think we're all living very lazy lives,' said Elfie, as she picked a climbing rose beside her and placed it in her belt; 'I feel as if every day here is one long holiday!'

'Well, we are not at school,' returned Clare; 'and I beg to state I have not been idle to-day. Attending to the flowers in the house every morning is no joke! I was nearly two hours over them; then I wrote letters and took them to the post before luncheon, and I have been mending a dress, and tidying my cupboards since.'

Gwen laughed a little derisively. 'You will never die of hard work, Clare.'

'I think it is harder work doing what I have done, than sitting still in the same chair from ten o'clock to one, and simply reading and writing!'

'Ted was asking for directions in the garden,' said Agatha, looking up; 'but when I peeped inside the study, Gwen, and saw you had one of your writing crazes on, I knew it was no good coming to you.'

'No, he has plenty of work, and I shall be occupied in the morning for some time now.'

'Why have you taken such a fit of it?' asked Clare. 'You're writing as if for your life.'

'I want money,' was the brief reply.

'What for?'

'That I shall not tell you at present. I want it so much, that I am even condescending to write silly stories, which I despise myself for doing.'

'Oh! that will be delightful,' exclaimed Elfie. 'Couldn't you read us one now, to pass the time?'

'I will read you a kind of conundrum I have dashed off this morning to amuse some sentimental goose like Clare!'

'Thank you,' said Clare imperturbably; and when Gwen sauntered into the house to get her manuscript, she said,

'Gwen is preparing some surprise for her family. You mark my words; before long she will unfold a startling plan of action!'

Gwen reappeared very soon, and settling herself in her easy chair, began to read in a lazy and slightly mocking tone as follows:—

'The princess walks in her garden alone. Her face is sad, and her steps are slow. She reaches a low moss-covered wall, and leaning upon it gazes dreamily and wistfully upon the busy crowded city below. Sounds of toil and labour meet her ears. The busy multitudes are all engaged in the various occupations of their spheres. And whilst the ringing laughter, the joyous mirth, of some is borne upwards by the breeze, it is mingled with the sobs and bitter weeping of the neglected and oppressed. Stretching out her soft white hands, she clasps them in piteous yearning.

'"My soul craves for it," she cries. "Since first I became conscious of its absence I am longing to find it. If I could devote a lifetime to it, and obtain it at last, I should die content!"

*   *   *   *   *   *

'She stands in the deepest recess of a lonely forest. Far away from the city, no human habitation is near. Her feet are on the moss-covered ground, soft as velvet to the touch. Above is a canopy of green, through which the pure blue heavens appear, and the rays of the setting sun are giving the stately elms and rugged oaks a golden beauty of its own. She is leaning against a copper beech, and her soft brown hair is kissing the shining bark. Her blue eyes are turned upwards, full of expectancy and hope. She stands like a beautiful statue. A squirrel darts up a tree close by, and rabbits sport amongst the fallen leaves. The birds are carolling forth their evening hymns of praise, and Nature seems to be parading its loveliness. But her face is sorrowful still, and she shakes her head dejectedly. "It is of no avail," she murmurs; "even here in such a scene I cannot obtain my heart's desire! I yearn more for it day by day, and yet with the crushing longing within my breast I seem further away than ever from it!"

'She turns, and retraces her steps to the home of her forefathers.

* * * * * *

'A luxuriously furnished apartment; cool and refreshing after the glare of the sun outside. The Venetian shutters are closed. Sweet-scented flowers are filling the room with their perfume. The sound of children's happy voices, as they roam through the meadows and play in the new-mown hay, the humming of bees, sipping their honey from the full-blown flowers, come in at the open windows. Upon a couch in the darkest corner of the room lies our princess. She is not asleep; her hands are folded listlessly across her breast, her lips are moving. Now burying her face in the cushions, she exclaims:—

"'No, I have it not. Methought I might find it even here. No happiness for me until I experience it All the gold I possess would I gladly give to have the exquisite pleasure of obtaining and realizing it!"

* * * * * *

It is night-time. She stands upon the summit of a hill alone, and her figure looks weird and ghostly in the silver moon-light. Her head is thrown back, her lips parted breathlessly; her whole attitude bespeaks eager and intense expectation.

She is waiting and watching for the desire of her heart.

'She overlooks the city, now wrapped in slumber. Green plains stretch away in the dim distance, and the moon throws its light upon her upturned face, making fantastic shadows around her. Hark! From yonder tree the nightingale trills out her midnight song. She listens and does not move, but hears it to the end. It ceases, and the wind rushes through the long grass at her feet, and shakes the leaves above, even venturing with its lawless impudence to buffet her fair brow, and scatter her brown locks across her eyes. A deep sigh escapes from her heaving breast. "It is hopeless. I am well-nigh despairing. Whither shall I go? I will not be conquered. I must find, and will find it soon!"

*　*　*　*　*　*

'Again we see her. In a grotto, deep in the heart of the earth. She is seated on a rock, and all is darkness save a faint ray of light that creeps through a small crevice overhead.

'No one is near. No living creature but herself, and she is still seeking and waiting for what she has not found. Water is trickling drop by drop from the moist roof above; the atmosphere is damp and close, yet little she heeds the discomfort of her surroundings, and heavy sighs come from her lips. She looks up at last, then wends her way still further into the innermost recess of the cavern. She stands beneath a deep vaulted roof, in deeper darkness, but in drier atmosphere, and here she pauses, a light coming into her sad blue eyes, and for the first time a smile hovering about her lips. A quiver of excitement, a thrill of suppressed awe vibrates through her nervously strung frame. "At last," she murmurs; "if nowhere else, I shall find it here."

'Her heart throbs violently, and in vain she places her hand upon it to still its beating. Moments pass in anxious hope, then suddenly she sinks to the ground in a passion of sobs and bitter weeping.

"'No, no, poor weak fool that I have been," she breaks forth, in disdainful self-contempt; "never in this life shall I obtain it, for outward circumstances influence it little. How vainly deluded I have been hitherto! Little did I imagine that the very longing and craving of my heart for it, would thereby prevent my possessing it!"

'She leaves the cavern, and returns to her home a wiser woman.'

Gwen folded her manuscript up quietly, adding indifferently, 'Now what was it she wanted?'

'I should say, "Work,"' remarked Agatha in her matter-of-fact way. 'She seems to have been a most idle young person.'

'Rest and contentment,' murmured Clare, looking at Gwen with dreamy, thoughtful eyes.

'Sleep, perhaps,' suggested Elfie.

'You're all wrong.'

'Tell us then.'

'She wanted silence.'

And humming an air, Gwen walked into the house without another word.

Elfie began to laugh. 'What a queer subject! Gwen never does write like other people. There is no moral at all.'

Neither of the others spoke for a little. Then Agatha said, folding up her work, 'It may take in certain magazines, but I think she writes far better when she keeps to facts, not fancies.'

'It has a moral,' said Clare, looking away over the meadows.

'What is it?' asked Elfie, regarding her curiously.

'Failure is in self, not circumstances!'

After which slow denunciation, Clare also moved into the house, and when she reached her bedroom she murmured to herself, 'And I know all my unrest and discontent come from within me. It is not my surroundings. Miss Villars must be right.'

CHAPTER VIII

ENTERTAINING A STRANGER

'In all things
Mindful not of *herself, but bearing* the burden of others.'

—*Longfellow*

It was Sunday evening. Agatha sat by the drawing-room window, her Bible on her lap, and her thoughts far away from things of earth. All the rest of the household were at church, and she was enjoying the stillness around her. The sun was setting just behind the pine trees in the distance, and shedding a rosy glow upon their slender stems; the hush of night seemed to be falling on all Nature, and Agatha was so wrapped up in her thoughts, that she did not notice the figure of a man quietly and swiftly approaching the house. She was the more startled when a voice broke upon the stillness; and she looked up to see a man standing close outside the window.

'Pardon me, madam, but will you kindly allow me to enter? I wish to have a few words with you.'

Visions of housebreakers, robbing, and perhaps murdering, if

Amy Le Feuvre

their wishes were denied them, flitted through Agatha's perturbed mind. She knew she was alone in the house, and beyond the reach of any help; she also realized that all the three French windows leading out to the verandah were open; but, nevertheless, she showed a brave front. Without rising from her seat, she looked the intruder straight in the face.

'Perhaps, if you will make known your errand, I will comply with your request. You are at present a perfect stranger to me.'

Her visitor smiled. He was an elderly man, with a stoop in his shoulders, and a rather shabby great-coat buttoned tight up under his chin.

'My errand might startle you,' he said; 'I wish to get at something in the study cupboard.'

Poor Agatha's heart beat loudly. 'That you cannot do without the owner's consent,' she replied sternly, 'and he is at present abroad.'

Then with a little old-fashioned bow the stranger took off his hat.

'No, madam, he is not abroad. He is before you!'

Agatha stared at him. She saw rather kindly-looking blue eyes peering at her through thick shaggy eyebrows; a care-worn, smooth-shaven face, with a very broad intellectual brow, and a smile that somehow or other disarmed her suspicions.

'Are you—are you sure?' she faltered stupidly.

'Sure that my name is Thomas Lester, and that instead of being a tramp or burglar molesting a lonely woman, I am now respectfully soliciting admission into my own house? Yes, madam, I assure you on the honour of a gentleman that I am no impostor!'

Agatha rose at once. 'Then please come in, and forgive my suspicions. I never heard of your return.'

'No,' he said, stepping inside and quietly taking a seat; 'I came back hurriedly, and did not wish my visit here to be known. That is why I chose to come down from London to-day, for I knew my respected brother would be safely and piously conducting his devotions in church. Have you made his acquaintance, Miss Dane?'

'No, he has not called upon us.'

'And you have seen nothing of my son? Do you know my story? I see by the book that you are reading that you must be a good woman. I know you are a brave one by my reception. May I confide in you a little?'

Agatha looked up sympathetically.

'We do know something about you,' she said; 'quite enough to make us feel very sorry for you.'

Mr. Lester then told her again much of what she had already heard, with additions, which drew out her sympathy still more for him. He told her that when he reached the farm where his son had been working, he found he had left it, saying he was going to track out his cousin, and would never come back till he had found him.

'My journey was fruitless, and then, after making many

useless inquiries, I fancied he might have returned home, as my last letter to him had urged him to be home again without fail before this summer would be over. So I came back, and find from my agents in London that he must be still abroad. My journey out there was a failure; both lads are swallowed up in the Australian bush, but I don't believe they are dead, and I am convinced that Alick will never come back without tidings of his cousin. Their affection for each other was absurd, preposterous, and utterly out of place.'

He paused, and Agatha asked anxiously:—

'Are you going back to Australia again?'

'I don't know.'

'Perhaps you wish to return here?'

'Not at all. I never will, until things are on a different footing between myself and my brother. He has insulted me openly in this neighbourhood; even daring to hint that I have plotted to get rid of his son! No, I came to get something I want out of my locked cupboard. I conclude you will have no objection to my doing this?'

'Certainly not'; and Agatha rose and led him to the study. She left him there, but as she turned away she heard him quietly lock the door behind her; and again she felt a nervous thrill run through her, as she wondered if he were an impostor after all.

Half an hour later he came back to her in the drawing-room.

'I am going to do a foolish thing,' he said; 'I cannot tell what impels me to do it, but the very thing I was going to take away I am deliberately going to leave here with you.'

'I would rather you took it away, whatever it is,' Agatha said hastily.

'It will not be in your way. I see you are careful tenants, and as long as you keep my wishes respected about that locked cupboard, it will be safe; far safer than if I carried it about with me, as I thought of doing. If you wish to correspond with me at any time, my agents in London will forward anything to me. I will give you their card. One thing I am going to leave with you, and this shows the confidence I place in you. It is the secret of opening that cupboard. I have sealed the directions up in this envelope; and I want you to give me your solemn promise that you will keep it as I give it to you, in trust for my son. When he returns, he will be sure to find his way down here. Be kind to him, and give him the envelope. I have never confided to him the secret of the cupboard, and I wish him to open it as soon as he arrives. It is most important he should.

'You may wonder at my trusting a comparative stranger with such a charge, but I am a good reader of faces, and I do not think you will fail me. Promise me you will keep this envelope from the knowledge of any one, even from your sisters; and promise me you will do what I desire about it!'

But,' objected Agatha, 'we may not live here always. If we leave before your son returns—'

'My son is bound to come back before the end of this year, if he is alive.'

'Then will he wish to come and live here?'

'No. Neither my son nor I will ever live here again, I fancy.'

'Then where will you be when your son returns?'

Amy Le Feuvre

'I do not know. In my grave, perhaps. I have told you my agents' address.'

So, after a little hesitation and a great deal of wonder, Agatha gave him her promise to act as he wished. Seeing he looked tired and worn, she asked him if he would have any refreshment, but he refused.

'You need not make my visit known throughout the neighbourhood,' he said, standing up and buttoning up his coat; then glancing at her Bible, which lay open on the table by her side, he added rather sarcastically:

'If you want a Bible study, Miss Dane, discover the answer to a proposition made in the Book of Jeremiah. I believe it's in the first verse of the twelfth chapter. You see I know my Bible well.'

'And so do I,' said Agatha, smiling, 'though not so well as I ought. And I can tell you that the same proposition troubled David; but he solved it in the sanctuary.'

'Is that a hint to me?' said Mr. Lester, a little taken aback by her quick reply.

'No; though don't you think it a pity to hold aloof from God's worship on the day set apart for it? Even the heathen are more respectful to their false gods.'

'I did not expect to receive a sermon here,' he responded, with a little dry smile.

'No, and I would not presume to give it,' said Agatha, smiling in her turn. 'And don't be surprised that I knew your verse in Jeremiah so well. I came across it the other day, and thought it fitted in well with a favourite Psalm of ours, the thirty-seventh. We have had an experience something like yours, and it would make one bitter sometimes, if one did not remember that our circumstances are being shaped by God Himself.'

Mr. Lester said nothing, but held out his hand, and Agatha took it, feeling strangely drawn to him. They shook hands, and then, as Mr. Lester stepped out into the verandah, he turned.

'Remember your promise, and offer a prayer sometimes for a disappointed old man who fears he won't live to see his hopes fulfilled.'

He disappeared in the fast-falling twilight, and Agatha sat in her chair, gazing before her as if in a dream. Her sisters found her strangely preoccupied when they returned; but when they were enjoying a cold supper together, and the maids were out of the room, she told them of her strange visitor, begging them to say nothing of it to any one, and purposely omitting to tell them of the envelope entrusted to her.

'Are you perfectly certain he was genuine?' said Gwen anxiously. 'It was a very risky thing to let him have sole possession of the study! Why did you not offer to stay in the room with him?'

'How could I? He locked himself in!'

'Worse and worse! He might have been taking impressions of the locks, and will break into the house another night by the study window!'

Agatha shook her head with a confident smile. 'He was a gentleman, and had a true face; I am not at all afraid of him.'

'It is quite an adventure,' said Clare, flushing up with excitement. 'Now, what do you think he wanted to get at in the cupboard? Is it a treasure store, or does it hide some ghastly secret? I really think I should have peeped through the key-hole, and seen how he opened it. It would have been such an opportunity.'

'Did you dismiss him with a tract?' asked Gwen mockingly.

'No, I had not one by me,' said Agatha simply. 'I feel very sorry for him. He is in great trouble about his son.'

'And you are sure he does not want to come back and turn us out? It would be very awkward if he did.'

'He seemed quite certain on that point.'

Gwen heaved a sigh of relief. 'I think I will tell you what I purpose doing, she said rather solemnly; 'or shall I put it off till to-morrow?'

"'Tis the Sabbath,'" quoted Elfie, mimicking old Deb Howitt's tones.

'If it is anything startling, I would rather you kept it till to-morrow,' said Agatha; 'I have had quite enough to startle me already.'

'Oh, very well,' responded Gwen unconcernedly; 'my news will keep.'

But she was disappointed that no one seemed curious enough to press her for more information, and the next day, after working hard all the morning in the garden, went off to see the Howitts in the afternoon.

Gwen had taken a real liking to the sisters, and would often drop in upon Patty, and have a cup of tea with her when her sister was away.

It was a warm day, and she was glad to reach the cottage, with its shady orchard round it, after the blazing meadows she had crossed.

Under an old apple-tree, on a low stool, she found Patty sitting, knitting furiously away at a grey worsted stocking, and muttering to herself as she did so.

'What is the matter?' Gwen asked gaily, as she took a seat on the grass by her side; 'you look quite agitated!'

"Tis one of our bad days,' said Patty, looking up and shaking her head dolefully. "Tis generally the wash-tub that does it, and Monday is our washing day. I did mean to be careful that my lips didn't offend, but 'tis no good when she's of an argumentative turn! Yes, miss, she's locked me out, and I hope she's enjoyin' herself, for on Mondays I always bakes a cake for tea. Deb never did have a light hand for such things, and she's a-messin' in there with my flour bin, and pilin' tons of coal on the fire, for I've been watchin' the smoke, and I can tell, and if I'm kept out here till dark, I'll maintain a promised wife comes before a sister!'

'Is that the discussion?' asked Gwen, her eyes twinkling with amusement.

'Now let me put it to you, miss, and she'd no business to begin it over the wash-tub, for it wants a cool head and a quiet mind to tackle such things. She was tellin' me of a case that was told her up at Thornicroft Manor, which is three mile the other side of Brambleton; and the housekeeper knew the parties concerned, being first cousin once removed to the

Amy Le Feuvre

young man. He was engaged to be married to an orphan girl, a-tryin' to earn her livin' by dressmakin', but makin' a very poor thing out of it. And they had kept company for six years, and then his mother died and left his only sister on his hands. But mind you, miss, they were a-goin' to be married, and had fixed the day before his mother took ill, and then what does the young fellow do but break it all off with his girl, sayin' he was only able to keep one woman, and that would have to be his sister! Now what do you think, miss? I say it was a cryin' shame of him, and Deb, she will have he did right, for his sister was delicate, and flesh and blood come first, she says. We argued it up and down, and she cried him up, and I cried him down, and we gets hotter and hotter. We couldn't keep off it after we left the wash-tubs and was a-havin' a bit of dinner; but I sticks to it that a promised wife comes first, and then, with a shove, I found myself out of doors, and the key locked behind me!'

Gwen laughed till the tears ran down her cheeks. Old Patty's intense interest in the unknown young couple, and her warm partisanship for the little dressmaker, together with her tragic tone and injured demeanour, were too much for her gravity.

'You are two foolish old women,' she said at last. 'I suppose it is love of your own opinions, and not the fate of these strangers, that makes you so combative. Which of you has the stronger will?'

'Ay, we're wonderful alike in temper, more's the pity, but I consider myself a fitter judge of right and wrong than Deb, who goes about and hears so much that it's all hearin' and no meditatin', whiles I sit here, and has the time and oppor-toonity to weigh the matters in and out, without the clack of many tongues to confuse my brain and make me say a man is a saint when he is a fool, not to say a sinner!'

Nothing that Gwen could say would calm the old woman, and when she went up to the cottage door, Deb remained conveniently deaf to all her knocks. She came home, and gave a graphic description of the quarrel to her sisters; but when their obstinacy was being condemned, Agatha said in her quiet way:

'Well, Gwen, you ought to have sympathy with them, for if any one ever goes against you, I am sure you feel as they do.'

'You mean I am fond of my own way and opinions, and won't bear contradiction! Oh, Agatha, how you love to preach to us all! I won't say you are mistaken, for I am not going to get up an argument, and I want you all to be especially agreeable while I lay a plan of mine before you.'

'Now for it,' murmured Clare; and both Agatha and Elfie leant back in their chairs, the one in anxious, the other in amused anticipation of what might follow.

Amy Le Feuvre

CHAPTER IX

GWEN'S RESOLVE

'How little thou canst tell
How much in thee is ill or well!
Nor for thy neighbour, nor for thee,
Be sure!'

—Clough

Gwen cleared her throat. She sat in a low wicker chair by the open window of the drawing room, and for a minute her eye wandered out into the back garden, which looked in perfect order, and hardly needed the incessant hoeing and weeding of a lanky youth, who was now resting on his hoe and leaning against the wall in a sleepy attitude.

'We have now been here three months, and after the satisfactory evening we had with our accounts, Agatha, last week, we have come to the conclusion that we can live here well within our income. This being the case, and all anxiety for the future—'

'You're talking like a book,' interrupted Elfie saucily; 'don't purse up your mouth so, and look so superior, and like

Cousin James.'

'Very well, then, I will come to the point at once. I mean to go out to California and pay Walter a visit, and I want to sail before the end of this month.'

There was a dead silence. Then Agatha said a little drily, 'And you will want your 100 pounds to do that, of course?'

'No, I don't.' Gwen's tone was a little sharp. 'I have some in hand from my writing. I can see from your faces that you don't approve, but I've had it in my mind for a long time, only I have waited to see how things would go. Cousin Jacob's treachery was a bitter blow, as I was afraid you would want me at home to look after you all—'

'We're not the poor fools you think us,' put in Clare indignantly.

Gwen went on as if she had not heard her: 'And now I have got the garden into such excellent condition, and you are all shaking down and finding friends and occupations for yourselves—Agatha, the vicar and the villagers; Clare, her sweet Miss Villars; and Elfie, divided between the church organ and her music at home—I shall not be needed or missed. I don't mean to be away for years, but I am sure from Walter's letters that he is not doing as well as he should. He wants shaking up, perhaps starting in a new groove; and, honestly, I want to see life in the Colonies. It will do me good, and I hope I shall do him good. I may be back in six months' time. That is my idea—to pay him a visit, and then come back to you here.'

'I suppose we should all like to visit him,' said Clare crossly. 'Why shouldn't one of us go, and you stay at home? I am sure a winter here will finish me.'

Walter seems such a stranger to us,' said Elfie, 'that I wonder if he will like it. He was always at a boarding-school, and we only saw him for the holidays, and then he went abroad directly he left school. I hardly know anything about him. Has he any idea you are going, Gwen?

'I will write by the next mail and tell him. I know him a little better than you do, Elfie, for you were but a child when he left England. He has often said how he would like one of us out there to keep house for him. Of course, he will be delighted.'

'I am sorry you want to go,' Agatha said slowly.

'Why? Is there any good reason why I should stay at home?'

Agatha was silent, and though the younger girls plied Gwen with innumerable questions, and were full of excitement about it, she said nothing, and presently walked out of the room.

Gwen looked after her with a mixture of doubtful perplexity and annoyance. She and Agatha had always been much together, and she valued her opinion, though determined not to be swayed by it. She felt this silence meant disapproval, and was by turns uneasy and indignant at it. It was not till after Clare and Elfie had retired to bed that night that Agatha referred to the matter. And Gwen little knew that she had been kneeling at her bedside praying for guidance in offering her advice, for more than an hour that evening.

'Well,' said Gwen, with a little laugh, as she reclined in her favourite wicker chair, and looked up at her sister's grave face, as she turned from her writing-table to speak, 'what does Madam Prudence say to my scheme?'

'I think it is too important a step to take hastily,' said Agatha.

'My dear, I have been thinking of it for months; there has been no haste in the matter. Removal of objection number one! Now for number two!'

'I think,' said Agatha slowly, 'that you are quite as likely to unsettle Walter as to settle him. He is not doing very grandly, but he keeps out of debt; and it seems to me that it is only by steady perseverance that fortunes are made nowadays. Then you may seriously inconvenience him by giving him such short notice of your intentions. A man living by himself on a small farm is not prepared to receive ladies at a day's notice. He may be away from home when you arrive. Oh yes, I know you are not going to be influenced by what I say, but I do ask you to look upon it as a serious matter. And, Gwen, you know I don't often "preach," as you term it, but I do wish you would practise the verse old Nannie gave you just before we left London. It is an important step. Do commit it unto the Lord.'

'I am not religious,' said Gwen, a little lightly.

'Do you never mean to be?'

'I don't know. Every one has a different nature. It is natural for you to be good. It is natural for you to trust and lean upon religion, because you have such a humble opinion of your own judgment and powers. Now I feel—I can't help feeling —a confidence in myself. It may be conceit, but it is natural for me to trust in my own judgment, and plan my own course of life, and until disaster attends my attempts I shall continue to act for myself. Of this I am certain!'

'Ah, don't say that!' exclaimed Agatha; 'it would be sad if disaster were to follow this step of yours. I hoped, from your

Amy Le Feuvre

advocating a country life, that you would be content to settle down here quietly. If it is the dulness of the place that is driving you abroad, I am sorry we ever came here.'

'I am never dull anywhere,' Gwen said quickly; 'I have too many resources. It is not that at all. I have wanted to go out to Walter for a long time, and now I have made enough money to do it, nothing will stop me.'

'You are so sure of yourself,' said Agatha, sighing.

'Yes, and I am not ashamed of it. We can't be all alike, and self-confidence is a great blessing sometimes. It saves one from an infinite amount of care and worry.'

Agatha was silent. As is often the case with sisters, there was great reserve between them on matters that lay closely to their hearts, and though Agatha longed to warn Gwen of her besetting fault, she hesitated.

Gwen continued with alacrity: 'I have made inquiries about steamers, and hope to sail the week after next. I have very little preparation to make, for I am not given to much luggage.'

'And you mean to go out quite by yourself?'

'Why not? In these days chaperons are unnecessary. There are always some nice people on board who befriend single women. I am not a young girl.'

'You are not very old,' said Agatha, scanning the bright, handsome face with its wilful mouth and determined chin; 'and as I know vanity is not a failing of yours, I may say that you are too good-looking to be going about the world alone.'

Gwen laughed. 'Oh, you poor old thing! Why will you try to mother us all, when you cannot manage it! You may be perfectly certain I can take care of myself. Now shall we go to bed, or have you any more objections to make?'

'I wish you would pray over it,' were Agatha's parting words; and when Gwen got to her room that night she pondered over them.

She was not actually irreligious. She read her Bible occasionally, and went through a form of prayer by her bedside every night; but religion had never touched her heart. It was but an empty name to her, and she was too secure in her self-confidence and pride to ever feel her need of anything outside herself.

She drew her Bible towards her now, and turned to the 37th Psalm. She first glanced at the verse Nannie gave her, then read the psalm through carefully and steadily.

'It exactly describes Cousin James,' was her inward thought. 'I wish we could always see the good righted in this life, and the wicked cut off. I am afraid I could not follow out these precepts in my life. It is all waiting and trusting and doing nothing oneself, but letting God do it all for one. It is a psalm that must bring wonderful comfort to Agatha. Of course, I shall be able to pray that my visit to Walter may be for good, but I am sure it will. It is not as if I am meditating some very wrong course of action. If they really wanted me here, I would not think of leaving them. I am going out for Walter's good. Oh dear! how often I wish I had been the man in our family!'

With such thoughts as these she presently bent her head, and asked a blessing on her undertaking, and then turned into bed, feeling very virtuous at having done so.

Amy Le Feuvre

There was a great deal of talk between the sisters about Gwen's proposal, but not one of them now thought to dissuade her, and the only unpleasant criticism she had to bear was from Miss Miller.

Elfie and Gwen met her in the village, and she stopped them at once.

'What is this I hear?' she demanded, tapping Gwen on the shoulder with her stick. 'Are you going off to find a husband abroad, because you haven't been able to pick one up here? I thought you young ladies would be disappointed when you came to know our neighbourhood.'

'Our friends and acquaintances are not limited to this small corner, Miss Miller,' retorted Gwen, holding her head proudly; 'we should be in a poor plight if they were. And if we felt dull, London is not out of reach. I am going out to my brother.'

'So I have been told. You are going to live amongst bushrangers and savages. It shows a refined and modest taste to go where you will be the only woman. But I am surprised at nothing in these days, when everything is topsy-turvy, and society at its worst. Women vie with one another in being conspicuous, and girls go about the world in men's clothes!'

Elfie began to laugh, but Gwen said haughtily,—

'Since it does not surprise you, Miss Miller, I wonder you mention it at all.'

'Husband-hunting!' growled Miss Miller; and she hurried past them without another word.

'She is an impertinent woman!' said Gwen wrathfully.

'I think she is an old dear,' said Elfie merrily. 'You never hear people speak out their thoughts as she does! I always wonder what she is going to say next. The other day I was leaving a message for Agatha at the vicarage, when she came out with Lady Buttonshaw, who had been calling there. She said good-bye to her, and then added with great severity: "It is a good thing for you to be without your maid for a little. I shall not hurry Emma Gray to go to you. A woman might as well turn into a fashion-block as allow her maid to clothe and unclothe her as your maid does you! Bestir yourself, my dear. Find out on which side the buttons on your boots are, and how many hairpins are necessary for the erection of your pretty hair!" Lady Buttonshaw only laughed as she walked away. I suppose everybody knows that her bark is worse than her bite!'

Gwen had a different criticism pronounced upon her departure by old Deb and Patty. She went to wish them good-bye, and their surprise was great when she told them where she was going.

'Is it among the wild beasts and heathens? Well, you're a brave young lady to venture out all alone. But I should be terribly afeared of losin' my way. Are there signposts all the way?'

'There, Patty, you ain't showin' off your knowledge to talk so! Miss Gwen will go all the way in a steamer, and her brother will be meetin' her when she comes to land. It's the steamers are so tryin' to flesh and blood. Mr. Giles told me all about it when he went to America with his master. You have to sleep on shelves up the wall, and there be no washin' your clothes for the whole time you're on the sea, which to a clean, decent body must be dreadful! And the food is shaken out of you as fast as you gets it down, and 'tis a marvel that a body gets to the other side o' the world alive!'

Amy Le Feuvre

'It's wonderful good of you, miss, to go to take care of your brother!' said Patty, regarding Gwen with an awe-struck face; 'but you gentlefolk seem to be hardier to such things than us should be. And then you'll be able to speak them foreign langwidges. But it's to be hoped the cannibals won't get hold on you. I've only seen one person come back from foreign parts alive, and that was Tom Clark, and he was a sailor. But I reckon there are a few beside him that live to come back!'

'You'll not be marryin' an Indian prince out there, miss?' put in Deb anxiously.

'Miss Gwen is a Christian,' Patty said solemnly. 'She wouldn't be marryin' a heathen who keeps wives by the score, and eats them up by turns!'

And Gwen laughingly assured them that she meant to return as she went—a single woman.

The days slipped by; Gwen, with her usual energy and determination, arranged for her journey in every detail, and when the time came, took leave of her sisters with cheerful equanimity.

'It is not for very long,' she said; 'and if you want me back sooner, you have only to wire and tell me so. I shall be back, I hope, before Christmas.'

But Christmas seemed to Agatha a long way off, and she perhaps of all the sisters felt most depressed at Gwen's departure.

CHAPTER X

CLARE'S DISCOVERY

'A closed bud containeth
Possibilities infinite and unknown.'

Life went on very quietly with the three who were left. Elfie
was the sunshine of the house; her ringing laugh and little
snatches of song, as she came in and out, cheered all who
heard her. And Clare, fitful and uncertain in her bright
moods, could not understand Elfie's unfailing good-humour.

'You never will take life seriously,' she said to her one
morning after breakfast, as they were waiting for the
postman in the garden, and Elfie had seated herself on the
top bar of the gate, swinging herself to and fro, and trilling
out an old English ditty as she did so.

'I can't make cares when we have none,' she responded
laughingly; 'I have never been so happy in my life as I am
now.'

'I wish I could be contented with so little.'

'Oh, you! You're always straining after shadows, and won't

live in the present at all. Now tell me, what have you to make you unhappy to-day? You're expecting a letter from Hugh, and Miss Villars is coming to tea with us this afternoon. Those are two pleasures for you. And then look at our weather! This is an ideal summer.

"Strange that summer skies and sunshine
Never seem one half so fair,
As when winter's snowy pinions
Shake the white down in the air."

Why don't you live in the present?'

'Don't preach,' said Clare carelessly; 'it's too warm this morning to argue. Here comes that lazy man at last!'

Elfie sprang down and seized the letters with a bright nod of welcome to the stolid-looking postman.

'Here is one from Gwen! Agatha will be pleased; and here is Hugh's! Now, Clare, be happy! And there is not one for me, so I shall go to Agatha to hear how Gwen is getting on.'

She darted into the house, and Clare, sinking into a chair on the shady verandah, prepared herself to enjoy one of Captain Knox's periodical epistles. They were always full of life and interest; and Clare was beginning to feel a sick longing to have him back with her again. Even as she read she let the letter fall in her lap whilst she mused upon the past. 'I used to be so cross to him. I took all his love and attention so coolly. If I only had him back again, how different I would be! He was always so unselfish, and I was so selfish and dis-contented. I can't think now how I could have been unhappy when I was constantly seeing him. Oh, Hugh! if you could come to me now, I would never grumble again! One touch, one word, one look, if only I could have it!'

And Clare's blue eyes filled with tears, and her sight was dim as she finished reading her letter. She remained motionless for some minutes then, and was rising slowly from her seat to go and hear the news of Gwen, when a slip of paper fluttered out of the envelope. It was a postscript as follows:—

'Here is Mr. Lester's motto on the carved scroll. It was in Arabic, as I thought, and the translation is something like this:—

'A closed bud containeth
Possibilities infinite and unknown.'

Clare folded it up with a sigh.

'There is no clue there, that I can see. I will have another look at the cupboard this afternoon.'

She joined her sisters, and heard a racy account of Gwen's experiences on board ship. She had fallen in with nice people—a Mr. and Mrs. Montmorency, going out to California for the third time to look after some property of theirs.

'We are great friends,' Gwen wrote. 'Mr. Montmorency is a clever, well-read man—can talk on any subject, and has been in California for nearly thirty years. His advice would be invaluable to Walter. I am asking them to come and pay us a visit when they are in our neighbourhood, which they hope to be before long, and they have promised to do so. Mr. Montmorency does not think farming pays in Walter's locality. He says there are many things more profitable; but I will not tell you all our talk. I spend most of my time with them. You may be interested in hearing that Clement Arkwright is on board. But I give him a wide berth. He asked

　　　　　Amy Le Feuvre

some rather impertinent questions the first time we spoke to each other. I showed him it would not answer, and now we pass each other with a bow!'

'Who is Clement Arkwright?' asked Elfie.

Clare laughed.

'One of Gwen's old admirers. He has too much of her self-will and dogged pride to pull with her. Do you remember, Agatha, how we used to enjoy their wordy combats? I always thought that at the bottom of all her antagonism to him she really liked him; but she never would allow it.'

'I dare say he wonders at her going out alone,' said Agatha musingly; 'she does not say where he is going. I remember he had a great idea of shielding women from the brunt of life, as he used to call it, and that was one thing that Gwen could not stand.'

'What more does she say?' asked Clare.

'Not much. She says she means to study farming while she is away, and hopes to get valuable hints from Mr. Montmorency, who seems to be a perfect mine of information.'

'One of Gwen's sudden friendships!' observed Clare. 'I only hope it will last out the voyage!'

She left the room and went to the study, where she spent the rest of the morning in trying to copy Mr. Lester's carving on the cupboard. She was very fond of this occupation, and had decorated several little tables and stools. She found Mr. Lester's handiwork a great help to her, and was ambitious of designing a cupboard herself, very much after the pattern of the study one.

As she was tracing a part of the delicate border edging the panels, she suddenly started, and the thought flashed across her:—

'It must be one of these buds that contains the secret of the lock or spring, and that is the meaning of the words:—

"A closed bud containeth
Possibilities infinite and unknown."

She passed her fingers over some thick buds that hung in festoons along the border, and then with finger and thumb she tried to move each one in succession. At last one began to revolve; she turned it breathlessly, and after three or four revolutions, a sharp click, and then the panel opened.

For one minute Clare stayed her hand—irresolute. She had discovered the secret, and the contents of the cupboard would be before her eyes.

Surprise, delight, and a little dismay were mingled in the discovery. Stories that Jane had told her of the mysterious cupboard that some thought contained proofs of a crime, came to her mind. The remembrance of the owner's express wish that it should remain locked, made her hesitate.

It was a battle between intense curiosity and the sense of honour; but the latter prevailed. Clare closed the panel hastily, turned round the carved bud till it was closed, and then walked to the window, turning her back on her temptation.

She heaved a sigh of relief.

'I am sure I deserve praise for such virtue. No one can taunt me with a woman's curiosity after this! Now the question is, shall I tell the others? I don't think I will. It wouldn't do to let the maids get wind of it. I shall write and tell Hugh, of course. How interested he will be! It was really rather clever of me to find it out, for it is a wonderfully ingenious device. And I suppose the old man never dreamt of women deciphering his Arabic characters, much less following the ambiguous hint given in his motto.'

And then sitting down at the writing-table, Clare commenced a letter at once to Captain Knox. Her discovery delighted her, and for the rest of the day she was sunshine itself.

Miss Villars arrived in the afternoon, bringing with her two shy, lanky girls of fourteen and fifteen.

'I knew you would let me bring two of my visitors,' she said aside to Agatha; 'they are recovering from influenza. Their father is a curate in Liverpool, and I am trying to feed them up, and get a little colour in their cheeks before they go home again. They are rather shy, but it is such a pleasure for them to be in the country.'

Elfie soon took possession of the girls, and wandered round the garden with them, where their tongues unloosed, and they poured forth such a flood of chatter that she had no difficulty in entertaining them.

'We are having such a lovely time. Miss Villars' house is like one you read of in books. We never thought we should ever stay in one like it. We feel as if we are in fairyland. You see, we are very poor, and only keep one servant, and there are seven of us at home, and our house is in a terrace, and smuts, and soot, and dust fly in at the windows all day long. Miss Villars is awfully nice, and she makes us enjoy ourselves. At home one feels quite wicked if one reads a storybook, because there are so many of the boys' stockings to be mended, and cooking, and our own lessons in between, for we go to a day school for three hours every morning. Now here, Miss Villars takes us out in the garden after breakfast under her shady trees, and puts one of us in a hammock, and the other in an easy chair, and leaves us there with some delicious books for a couple of hours. And then we see a dainty lunch coming out to us about eleven o'clock, and we drive and play tennis, and she treats us just like she might her own sisters!'

Elfie, looking at the radiant faces and sparkling eyes of the two delicate girls, envied Miss Villars the privilege of being able to bring such brightness and happiness into others' lives.

Meanwhile Clare was having a private talk with her friend, for after tea Agatha had sped down to the village on one of her benevolent errands.

'Have you found the true secret of happiness yet?' asked Miss Villars presently. 'You look brighter than when I last saw you.'

'I may be brighter now, but I shall have one of my black moods again soon. No, Miss Villars, I don't think I shall ever be satisfied in this life. The more I have, the more I want, and you couldn't expect me to be happy with Hugh in Africa!'

She laughed as she spoke, but her smile soon died away.

'I want him back dreadfully, Miss Villars. I never dreamt I would miss him so much; and I have a horrible feeling that he will not come back at all. I think I should die if he did not! I long sometimes to go out to him. But I can't. I must just wait, and I hate waiting! I never could wait for anything when I was a child, and it drives me nearly wild!'

Amy Le Feuvre

Clare spoke with such vehemence and passion that for a moment Miss Villars thought it best not to speak. Then she said slowly,—

'Poor child! you take life's lessons hardly. And I can't help you except by sympathy. There is only One who can, and you will not go to Him for the patience and rest of soul you need.'

Tears filled Clare's blue eyes. She gazed away out of the window up to the sweet summer sky, and her face grew wistful and sad.

'I am seeking Him,' she said in a low voice, 'but it all seems dark, and the Bible seems no help, and prayer a weariness; and then I give up trying, and try to amuse myself, and make the time pass as best I can.'

Then Miss Villars did a thing which Clare owned to herself that no one else but Miss Villars could have done naturally. She took hold of Clare's hand, and with closed eyes and bent head began to pray.

A very short and simple prayer, but a strange thrill ran through Clare as she realized this was indeed speaking to One who was close to them. And nothing jarred her feelings. She only seemed to be drawn into the very presence of her Saviour, who with open arms was waiting to receive and bless her.

When Miss Villars ceased speaking, Clare's head still remained lowered, and there was perfect silence. It was broken by Elfie's return from the garden with the girls; and without a word Clare crept softly away up to her own room, and Miss Villars left without seeing her again.

But up in her room Clare was kneeling by her bedside in a passion of tears.

'O God, help me, help me! I want to be right with Thee, I want this rest of soul; give it to me. Oh, if Thou art waiting to bless, I am ready, I am willing. Forgive me and save me for Christ's sake. Amen.'

She had never prayed so earnestly before.

Amy Le Feuvre

CHAPTER XI

AGATHA'S LEGACY

One by one, bright gifts from Heaven,
Joys are sent thee here below;
Take them readily when given,
Ready, too, to let them go.'

—Adelaide Procter

'Why, Agatha, what is the matter? You look quite scared! No bad news by the post, is it?'

Elfie asked the question one morning as she came into the dining-room to breakfast, and found Agatha staring out of the window with troubled eyes, and letting the brass kettle boil over on the white tablecloth with the greatest indifference.

She turned round and faced Elfie with pale cheeks.

'Mr. Lester is dead. It seems so sudden. He caught cold and died on the voyage out to Australia. And his lawyer writes to tell me about it.'

Elfie looked startled.

'Must we turn out of the house?'

'That is the strange part of it. The lawyer says he had a visit from Mr. Lester before he went, in which he informed him he was going to leave this house to me unconditionally, and a codicil has been added to his will to that effect.'

'Why, Agatha, I can hardly believe it! He must have fallen in love with you on the spot. Whatever induced him to think of such a thing?'

'I am sure I don't know, unless he was afraid of his cupboard. When I say he leaves the house to us unconditionally, that is the only condition he makes, that we live in the house and keep that cupboard locked till his son returns, and then let him have the contents. He told the lawyer he had left it to me as a trust, and he knew I was a woman of honour, so he would have no anxiety about it. And in return for this he bequeaths to us the house for good and all. I wonder what his son will say to it, if he ever does come back! I hardly know what to do about it. It seems so very extraordinary!'

But, extraordinary as it was, Agatha found on further correspondence that it was a fact. The house was legally bequeathed to her; and, after the first excitement of it was over, she thanked God with all her heart that she had now a certain dwelling. She had a great dislike to change, and was so wedded to the country round her, and had made so many friends amongst the poor, that it had been a secret dread for a long time that the owner would return, and they would have to move. She was telling Elfie something of the relief it was to her, when the latter remarked,—

'Ah, well, Agatha, Nannie's text for you is true: "Trust in the

Lord, and do good; so shalt thou dwell in the land, and verily thou shalt be fed!" You are provided for, at any rate.'

'And don't you find your verse true, too?' asked Agatha quietly.

Elfie coloured a little, then laughed.

'Yes, I do; but life is so pleasant that I have had nothing to put my happiness to the test.'

'And I hope it never need be,' was Agatha's response.

Not long after this Agatha was surprised by a visitor one afternoon, and this was no other than Major Lester.

He bowed stiffly to her when she entered the room.

'I have heard from my lawyer that the strange report flying about this neighbourhood is true,' he began abruptly. 'You will excuse my coming to you to make a few inquiries, but had you any acquaintance with my poor brother before you came here?'

'None whatever,' was Agatha's prompt reply.

'Then he is a perfect stranger to you?'

Agatha hesitated; then she said slowly,—

'I do not suppose it will matter now my mentioning it, but Mr. Lester came here about a month ago.'

Major Lester looked astonished.

'I was unaware that my brother had been in England at all

since his visit abroad; but he always was most erratic. And may I ask why his visit was to be kept a mystery?'

'I don't think there was any mystery about it. He simply asked me not to mention it.'

'Did he leave no message for me? May I ask his errand?'

'He left no message.'

Agatha was dignity itself. She was going to reveal nothing more, and Major Lester saw as much, and resented it accordingly.

'Well, I see you and my brother came to some understanding together; and, I suppose, this freak of his is the result.'

Then, pulling himself up, as he felt his temper was getting the better of him, he added, more blandly, 'Pray do not think I object to you as permanent neighbours. If I had any ladies in my household, they would have called on you before this. I came to you this morning because there is a locked cupboard of my brother's, which, as his nearest relative, I presume I have a right to open. I believe there are family papers in it of great importance. Perhaps you will kindly allow me to go into the study at once, as I am rather pressed for time.'

'I am sorry to have to refuse you, Major Lester, but I promised your brother that that cupboard should remain closed till his son came to open it.'

Major Lester glared at her, but Agatha maintained her quiet composure.

'He must have been as mad as a hatter!' he muttered; then

turned angrily to her.

'And may I ask when my nephew is to be back, as you seem fully conversant with the affairs of our family?'

'I do not know. Your brother thought he would return this year. Have you heard anything of your son?'

'My son has met his death by the hands of my nephew, at the instigation of his father! I warn you, Miss Dane, you may suffer the penalty of the law by refusing to let me have access to that cupboard. It is a mere question of time. If my nephew does not return soon, I shall insist upon having it opened, and I shall bring a lawyer with me to enforce my authority! I will not detain you longer now. Good-morning!' And Major Lester took his leave literally trembling with passion; so Agatha told her sisters afterwards.

'It is very unpleasant for us,' she added; 'I feel quite anxious lest Major Lester should insist upon having his way.'

'Have you nothing in writing from Mr. Lester himself about it?' asked Clare; 'I thought the lawyer sent you a written statement by him.'

'Yes, I have that; and, after all, the house is mine, and I suppose that includes the cupboard.'

'Of course it does. What did Mr. Lester say about the cupboard?'

'That it was not to be opened till his son came; and in this paper he bequeaths to me a certain portfolio of his that is in it. He says I can make what use I like of the contents. But of course I shall not get that till his son appears.'

'It is very romantic altogether,' said Clare; then, trying to speak indifferently, she added: 'Does Major Lester know how to open the cupboard, Agatha? I fancy it is not a very easy task.'

'I don't know,' said Agatha; 'perhaps he does not. In that case it is safe.'

And she thought with satisfaction of her sealed envelope safe at the bottom of her dressing-case. 'Well,' she added, after a pause, 'I am not going to worry over it. One must just do what is right, and leave the result.'

'But,' said Clare dreamily, 'supposing there is a hidden crime in that cupboard—papers that tell of the whereabouts of Major Lester's son—should we be right in keeping it hidden? Supposing I were to find a way to open that cupboard, Agatha, should I be wrong in doing it?'

Agatha looked startled.

'What do you mean? Are you trying to open it, Clare? I should hope you would not be so dishonourable. It is given as a charge to us. In fact, it is the condition of our keeping this house. And do you think anything would make it right for us to betray such a trust? I know an honest, upright man when I see him, and Mr. Lester was that, whatever Major Lester may be!'

Clare laughed a little confusedly.

'You are getting quite excited. I never said I intended opening it. I wish this wandering son would come back. Couldn't we advertise for him?'

Their conversation was here interrupted by another visitor,

and this was Miss Miller.

She came hurriedly and breathlessly in, pulling out the bows of her bonnet-strings, which was a way of hers when excited.

'Miss Dane, what is the meaning of this? No; I cannot stay to sit down. I'm off to a committee meeting in Brambleton, for the "Friendly Girls." The pony cart is waiting at the top of the lane. I have just met Major Lester. He is terribly put out by his visit here. Would not tell me particulars, but said you were siding with his nephew, who was hiding from the hands of justice, and refused him admittance into his brother's study. You are new-comers, my dear, and this will not do. How did you get acquainted with Mr. Lester? The major says he has been paying you secret visits. Very improper—single young women cannot be too careful. Why have you been keeping it a mystery? And what is it all about? And what is the secret of this mysterious cupboard?'

'That I cannot tell you, Miss Miller,' said Agatha, answering only the last of her questions; 'for I do not know it myself.'

'But you know something! We are not accustomed to mysteries here, and the major is an upright man, and a regular churchgoer, and his brother was a ne'er-do-well, But we won't say anything against him now, poor man! Only I assure you, you will make yourselves the talk of the neighbourhood if you three unmarried women scrape acquaintance with his son, and espouse his cause with such hot vehemence!'

'Miss Miller,' said Clare, with burning cheeks, 'you have no business to say such things of us; we have given you no cause to do so!'

Miss Miller just nodded her head up and down excitedly.

'I say just what I like, my dear, and no one is to dictate to me as to my manner of speech, least of all a young chit of a girl who knows nothing of life!'

Then Elfie came to the rescue, whilst Clare flounced out of the room in great indignation.

'Don't be cross with us, Miss Miller,' she said, in her pretty coaxing way. 'Major Lester left us when very angry, and you mustn't believe all he said about us.'

But Miss Miller would not be appeased, and she left very soon, declaring that it was all very 'strange indeed, and most mysterious,' and that 'people who could not be straight-forward, and made their own plans without reference to their spiritual guide, were a great trial to have in the neighbour-hood!'

'It really seems,' said Agatha, with a weary sigh, 'that Mr. Lester's legacy will prove anything but a blessing! I do wish people would leave us alone.' But a short time afterwards Major Lester's wrath and Miss Miller's strong partisanship in his cause were quite eclipsed by a greater trouble.

Agatha took in *The Times,* and it was generally delivered at their house about twelve o'clock in the morning, by the postmistress's little boy, directly he came home from school.

One morning Clare met him at the gate, and opened it herself. She was feeling anxious and uneasy. For the first time Captain Knox had missed the mail, and she was full of gloomy forebodings.

Agatha was tying up some straggling rose branches in the verandah, and Elfie practising away in the drawing-room.

Amy Le Feuvre

'Any news, Clare?' Agatha asked carelessly.

There was no answer. She looked up. Clare slowly came towards her, paper in hand. She was in a fresh white dress, with a bunch of crimson roses in her belt, her golden hair shining in the sun, but her face was as white as her dress itself, and she stared at Agatha as if she did not see her. Agatha dropped her hammer and nails with a crash to the ground.

'What is it, Clare? anything about Gwen?' she asked, in frightened tones.

Clare handed her the paper without a word, and still gazed before her, as if she were in a dream.

Agatha soon found it. Only a terse, short telegram, mentioning that reports of a massacre of a surveying party had just reached the African coast, and it was feared that none had escaped alive.

Captain Knox's name was amongst those of the party.

'It is only a report,' faltered Agatha.

'I know it is true,' said Clare steadily; and then she passed Agatha by, and went up to her room.

She locked her door, and seated herself in an easy chair by her window with the calmness of despair.

'He is dead, he is murdered, and he will never come back! I shall never see him again, and my life is at an end with his!'

These thoughts burnt themselves into her brain.

She leant out of her window, and gazed over the sunny meadows, noticing the smoke appearing from Patty's chimney, and a flock of swallows flying through it. Then she watched the motions of a frisky colt in the next field, and wondered if life seemed one long bright holiday to him.

And then crushing her roses up in one hand, she flung them out of the window.

'What are roses and sunshine to me now?' she thought passionately, her whole soul swelling in protest at the black cloud enveloping her. 'What a bitter mockery this peaceful scenery is, when one remembers the awful fate that has fallen on Hugh and me!'

And then bending her head in her arms, she laid them on the low window-sill, and sobs began to come that shook her from head to foot. Dry, tearless sobs they were at first, and she got up and paced her room in hot rebellion.

'It is cruel—cruel of God! He does not care! He might have let me have him back, when I was trying to be a true Christian! Such an awful death! Oh, Hugh, Hugh! my heart is broken!'

She seized hold of a cabinet photo that stood on her dressing-table. It was Captain Knox in his regimentals; and as his frank, fearless gaze met hers, the flood of her tears was loosed, and they came thick and fast, relieving her brain, but exhausting all her strength by their vehemence. Luncheon time came, but no one could get her out of her room, and Agatha wisely let her alone. At five o'clock she tried her door again, and this time Clare unlocked it, and met her on the threshold with tumbled hair, flushed face, and defiant eyes.

Amy Le Feuvre

'What do you want? Can't you leave me alone?'

'Oh, Clare darling, how I wish I could comfort you! You will be ill if you don't take any food. Will you not have a cup of tea?'

Agatha's eyes were red with crying, and her lips quivered as she spoke. She laid her hand gently on Clare's arm, but it was shaken off, and Clare turned her back upon her and walked to the window.

Then she burst forth passionately.

'I am not surprised! I knew when he went he would never come back again. I believe it is this house that is a curse to us! I always felt from the first night we entered it that it would bring us trouble; and why I am to be the victim I don't know! I hate and loathe it! Leave me alone. You needn't be afraid of my starving myself. I wish I could; but I have got to live, and I shall have to drag through it as best I can. There is no chance of my dying of a broken heart. People never do. I shall outlive you all, I expect. What are you waiting for? Do you want me to come downstairs?'

'No, I have some tea for you here.'

And Agatha disappeared, to bring in a dainty little meal on a tray.

As she put it down she said slowly: 'I wonder if you know where to take your trouble, Clare? God Himself will comfort you, if you let Him.'

'You needn't waste your breath in uttering platitudes, Agatha. I know that is the correct thing to say, but it doesn't do me an atom of good.' And Agatha left her with a sigh, and went to her own room to pray for her, and to ask that her trouble should soften, and not harden, her heart against the only Comforter.

CHAPTER XII

OUT IN CALIFORNIA

'A woman will, or won't, depend on't;
If she will do't, she will, and there's an end on't.'

On the wooden verandah of Walter Dane's ranch in Southern California sat Gwen one evening, enjoying the orange-flamed sunset in front of her. And lounging opposite her, smoking his pipe, was Walter—a good-looking young fellow, whose usual expression was supreme good-humour, but whose brow now was furrowed with anxious thought.

'You see, Gwen,' he said, knocking the ashes out of his pipe, and ramming in a fresh supply of tobacco in a slow, meditative fashion, 'it has been very good of you to come out and look me up. I've been longing for a sight of my own flesh and blood for years, and if I was only a sight better off, I'd offer you a home for good.'

'That I would not take, with many thanks,' said Gwen, laughing. 'Now come, ever since I arrived I have seen you have had something on your mind, so unburden! What is it?'

Walter looked across the great sweep of uncultivated ground

outside his ranch to the landmark of another ranch in the distance—a windmill which pumped up the water necessary for use from a great depth below.

'You saw the Setons yesterday. What did you think of them?'

As he asked the question he pulled at his heavy moustache rather nervously.

'I thought they were wonderfully nice people for colonials. The girl is a pretty little thing.'

'They are not colonials,' her brother returned quickly; 'at least, not more than I am: for they haven't been in this country as long. Meta only came out a couple of years ago. She was educated at home in Brighton.'

'Was she?'

Gwen was looking at her brother with keen eyes now. There was silence for a minute, then Walter said in a very quiet voice,—

'We have been engaged, she and I, for a twelvemonth, and the wedding is fixed some time next month.'

Another dead silence, then Gwen said, with a little laugh, 'Well, I am surprised. I did not think you were a marrying man. You never gave us a hint of this in your letters home.'

'No; for I foresaw a long engagement, and thought it might be deemed rash.'

'And how do you intend to support a wife?'

'I can manage it now. My ground is improving. The great

difficulty in this part of the country is want of water, and I have overcome that. Of course, it will be hard work for some time yet, but Meta knows what the life will be like, and an aunt in England has lately died, and left her a legacy. She does not come to me portionless!'

Gwen gazed in front of her with compressed lips. She would not show her consternation and discomfiture to her brother, though to herself she was saying, 'I made a mistake in coming out to him!'

Aloud she said,—

'Well, I suppose I must congratulate you. And I will not stay out here after your marriage; you will have one of your family at the ceremony, which ought to comfort you.'

'You will like her as a sister, will you not?' asked Walter, with anxiety in his eyes, as he turned and faced his sister.

'Oh yes. I thought she was a nice little thing. Not much character, I suppose; but you men prefer that style of woman. She struck me as a lady.'

'Rather!' And with a short laugh Walter put his beloved pipe in his mouth, and with a sigh of relief at getting through his news, sank into a lounge chair, prepared to give his full confidence to his sister, now that the worst was over.

But Gwen disappointed him by rising carelessly from her seat.

'I am very tired. Your early hours here make the day inter-minable. Good-night.'

She passed into the house humming the air of a song, but

once in her room her expression changed.

'He will marry and have a large family, and only just make his farming pay to support them all. He has no ambition, no desire to make his fortune and come back to England. It means a thorough colonial life for always. Oh, what fools men are!'

She paced her room with clenched hands.

'I never dreamt of such a thing. I came out here to shake him up, to make him better himself. And I find he is perfectly content, and considers my coming a decided nuisance, though he doesn't like to say so. He can barely afford to live comfortably himself, and yet he meditates a speedy marriage. I should like to postpone it. I suppose if I asked him to let me stay out here for three or four months and let his marriage wait till after I left him, he might agree, but then what should I gain by that? I want him to give up this farming, which will never make his fortune; but if he has a wife in view he will cling to it! How I wish he had heard Mr. Montmorency talk of the certainty of finding fresh gold-fields, if only men of push and a certain amount of money could be forthcoming! I will not let my journey out here be all in vain! Walter must be roused, and made to do some-thing better with his life than his present existence. I wish Mr. Montmorency would pay us a visit soon. He would advise him for his good. He says this country is teeming with riches under the surface, only colonists are often content with so little that they do not develop half the resources so close to them. After all, it won't hurt that girl to wait another year longer. She looks a simple, stupid little thing; and if Walter can be got to postpone his marriage, we may be able to do something with him yet.'

As Gwen thus cogitated, the scene in the cottage garden at

Amy Le Feuvre

home came before her, when she found Patty Howitt locked out by her irate sister, and her words flashed across her with clear distinctness now,—

'If I'm kept out here till dark, I'll maintain a promised wife comes before a sister!'

A shadow crossed Gwen's determined face at this recollection.

'It is not a case of me or the promised wife,' she muttered to herself with a little laugh. 'I would willingly go home again at once and leave the young couple to themselves, but it is of their future that I am thinking; and they will thank me in the end for it, I know.'

Not a doubt crossed her mind of the wisdom or expediency of trying to upset her brother's plans and purposes. She knew what influence she possessed over him. His was a placid, rather weak nature, true and steadfast in his dealings with others, and quite capable of holding his own as long as he kept in a certain groove; but for a man he was strangely uncertain and distrustful of himself, and one who always found it easier to take advice than to give it.

Gwen had a restless night. Her head was full of plans, and when the next morning there was a stir outside the house, and she was told that a 'strange gentleman and lady' had arrived, she was quite enough versed in colonial ways to show no surprise when she went out upon the verandah and greeted 'Mr. and Mrs. Montmorency.'

Walter was a capital host, and was genuinely pleased to see any friends of his sister. And Gwen felt that fortune had indeed favoured her, and sent to her aid the very one who could help best at this crisis.

Mr. Montmorency inspired most people with confidence, and it was not long before he was deep in discussions of the country with Walter, telling him many valuable facts about agriculture that had come under his own observation, and from that drifting on to talk of the mineral wealth that had as yet hardly been touched.

He remembered the gold rush in Northern California, and prophesied the same would take place in the part they were in. Walter listened, but said little, and even when Mr. Montmorency went on to unfold a scheme of his shortly to be put into project, he showed little interest.

'It is very well for men of means to venture on such under-takings. It wants capital, and there are few about here who would risk their hardly-earned savings on a speculation which might fail.'

Then Gwen, with her clear head and quick brain, took the matter up. Even bright little Mrs. Montmorency could talk well on the subject, and for the next few days little else was mentioned but a certain region a few hundreds of miles away, where Mr. Montmorency intended to begin operations, and where he had already found proof enough of the existence of gold to make it worth his while to start a company and set to work in earnest.

The next mail that left for England contained the following letter from Gwen to Agatha;—

'DEAREST AGATHA,—

'This is purely a business letter, and a very important one. I have told you all about Walter and his surroundings already, so will not go into that again. Mr. Montmorency has been staying with us. He is a clever, able man, very well connected, a nephew of Lord D—, and has spent most of his life out here. He is starting a company for working a gold-mine in this neighbourhood. There is a certain prospect of its being a grand success. I send you a bundle of prospectuses and papers, which I want you to look carefully through. I know how cautious you are where investments are concerned, and, of course, one cannot be too careful. You will see the directors are all wealthy men, and their names well known at home. Show the papers to old Mr. Watkins if you like, and if you're afraid of acting without legal advice. Now I come to the point. Mr. Montmorency has taken a great liking to Walter. He says he is too good to rust in this part as he is doing, and waste the best years of his life in slaving to earn a livelihood, with no prospect of anything better in years to come. And he has asked him to join him in his undertaking, and become an active partner in the concern. I won't waste time by going into it all, but it is a grand chance for Walter, and he is certain to make his fortune. The one condition is that he must have capital to invest. He is going to sell his farm, but that will not bring in much. What I propose is that we four should invest our capital in this. Hand it over to Walter, and then Mr. Montmorency will be able to take him into the concern. We shall not lose, but be gainers by this. Mr. Montmorency can assure us 5 per cent. interest from the first, and that is more than we are getting now. There is not the slightest risk or speculation in the matter, and Walter is fortunate to have found such a friend in Mr. Montmorency. I have already promised my portion. Talk it over with Clare and Elfie, and show them that it will not only be benefiting themselves, but will be the making of Walter.

'I must tell you that he is engaged to be married to a very nice girl out here, and she is going to invest a legacy of hers in the same company. Every one round here has the greatest confidence in Mr. Montmorency. He is still staying with us, and Walter quite enjoys his society. If you want any more information about the company, you can get it by applying at their office in London. I do hope, for Walter's sake, that you will not be long in making up your minds. It seems so wonderfully fortunate that I should have come out in the same steamer with the Montmorencys. The mail is going. I must stop. If Walter gets the capital he needs, he will go off with Mr. Montmorency to the centre of operations next month, and I shall then return home. I may tell you that he was thinking of getting married shortly, but he and Meta Seton have wisely settled to postpone it until he has a good income. I believe myself that he will soon be a rich man. If he is, I shall be well repaid for my journey out here. Love to all. Will write again soon.

'Your affectionate sister,
'GWEN.'

CHAPTER XIII

HIS LAST MESSAGE

I hold it true whate'er befall,
I feel it when I sorrow most:
"Tis better to have loved and lost
Than never to have loved at all.'

—Tennyson

This letter reached Agatha soon after the sad news had come to Clare of Captain Knox's death. At first his relatives hoped there might be some mistake, but when further details came to hand, they corroborated the first tidings received, and some weeks after his baggage was sent home, and as much information was given to his sorrowing relatives as could be gleaned from the one or two survivors of the fated party.

His mother wrote kindly to Clare, and gave her as much information as she had herself received, but that was not much. The little party had been surprised one day when out surveying, and were shot down one after the other by an unfriendly tribe who surrounded them. Two escaped to tell the tale, but when a punitive force was sent out at once, there were no signs of the fray. The enemy had carried off the bodies of their victims, and escaped beyond the reach of justice.

For days Clare was almost beside herself with grief, and in despair Agatha sent over for Miss Villars.

'She is so fond of you, that you may be able to comfort her as we cannot,' said Agatha, when Miss Villars promptly arrived on the scene. Miss Villars shook her head sadly.

'No human comfort is of much use in a case like this,' she said; but she went upstairs, and remained two hours with Clare, and when she left Clare begged her to come to her again.

'You do me good. You make me think there is a God, after all. I have been doubting everything. I feel it is a judgment on all my discontent and bad temper. I often used to tire of him, and wish he were different; and now I feel it would be heaven itself to see him standing before me as he used to do!'

To her sisters Clare preserved a stolid, impassive demeanour. She would not leave the house for three weeks after the tidings had come, and then unfortunately meeting Miss Miller, she was subjected to questionable sympathy.

'Very glad to see you out, my dear. Why haven't you been to church lately? It's a very bad sign to keep away from the means of grace when in trouble. Have you heard the particulars of Captain Knox's death? I hope you are quite certain about it, you seem to have gone into mourning very quickly. In cases like this there are often mistakes made. Was the body identified? Well—well, I am very sorry for you; but you would have felt it more if you had been his wife!'

Clare turned and fled from her, and stayed away from church for a month longer, then only going at Agatha's most earnest request.

When Gwen's letter was received, and Clare heard the contents, she said listlessly,—

'Walter can have my money if he likes; it will make no difference to me. You can write to Mr. Watkins, and get him to see to it, Agatha.'

'And mine, too,' put in Elfie brightly. 'Gwen has a good head for business, and if she is going to venture hers, I am sure we can ours.'

But cautious Agatha shook her head, and spread the papers out before her with a grave and anxious face. Then she disappeared for a short time. She knelt at her bedside and asked for guidance about such an important step. And when she rose from her knees she thought sadly that Gwen had planned and purposed without prayer, and wondered if she were too intent upon her own schemes to be wise in her judgment and decisions.

'I am going up to town to talk it over with Mr. Watkins,' she announced, a short time afterwards. 'I do not wish to be ill-natured, and selfish, and prevent Walter from getting on, but I have a horror of these gold-mining companies; and if it should come to a crash, we should literally have nothing left. Of course, you must do as you please, only don't act hastily. Let me hear what Mr. Watkins says.'

So to town she went, and came back very tired, but quite decided in her own mind. Mr. Watkins had not scoffed at the company. He had heard a good deal about it, and had clients who were taking shares in it. He thought it might prove a very good speculation, and there were sound business men backing it up. 'But,' said Agatha, 'he said most emphatically that it was a speculation, and that no one could be positively certain of its success; and, after a great deal of consideration, I have made up my mind to have nothing to do with it.'

'Did Mr. Watkins advise your not having anything to do with it?' asked Elfie.

'No; he was quite neutral. He would not commit himself either way.'

The result was that Clare and Elfie transferred their capital to Mr. Montmorency's company, trusting entirely to the assurances of the prospectuses that their dividends would be paid within the first twelvemonth.

And Agatha had the unpleasant task of writing her refusal to Walter, who had written by the same mail as Gwen, painting his future in glowing colours, and loud in praise of Mr. Montmorency.

'Clare,' said Elfie one afternoon, coming into the study, where Clare was reading in a dreary manner, 'come and see Deb and Patty with me, will you? Agatha wants some honey, and we haven't seen anything of them for ages!'

Clare put down her poetry-book with a sigh, but said she would go, and they were soon sauntering over the meadows to Beehive Cottage, as it was called by the villagers.

They found both sisters at home, and Deb was busy remaking two merino skirts for herself and Patty.

"Tis not very often I do dressmakin' at home, but we're gettin' rather shabby, and so I'm turnin' our Sunday bests. Sit

Amy Le Feuvre

down, young ladies, and Patty will get you a glass o' milk.'

'And how is your sister gettin' on over the sea?' asked Patty, when she had brought the milk and taken a seat opposite her visitors. 'Deb and me often wonders of her, and how she be likin' it.'

'Oh, she is all right—very busy, making us send our money out to invest in a gold-mine.'

'To buy a gold-mine!' ejaculated Deb.

'No; to put our money in it.'

'Ay; why the need for buryin' it down so deep? The earth is everywhere; it be a safe bank, 'tis true, but safer close to one, than in furrin parts, it seems to me.'

Patty spoke emphatically in her breathless manner; and Elfie laughed outright.

'No, she doesn't want us to bury it. We have taken shares in a company that is working the gold-mine.'

Deb and Patty shook their heads doubtfully over this statement.

'The company pickin' up gold is generally a low, bad set,' said Deb. 'I heard tell at Squire Johnson's of a young gentleman who was nigh murdered by a rascally set of men, and all because of gold in his pocket. Gold ofttimes brings a curse, my dears; 'tis best to spend as you goes. And if so be as you put a little by for your burial, well, the earth won't tell tales, and a flower will mark the spot. Did I ever tell you o' my great-gran'mother's money pot?'

'No,' said Clare, with interest, for any old tale delighted her; 'tell it to us now.'

'Great-gran'mother were livin' alone, and gran'mother, she were married four mile off, and used to come in on market days, and see the old lady. Great-gran'mother, she were rather snappy and short, and one day she says to gran'mother, "Sally, my girl, when you come to want, pull up a yaller marigold by the roots"; and gran'mother, she laughs, and says she, "What old wife talk be that, mother? Do marigolds bring luck?" Great-gran'mother, she died soon after, and gran'mother were sore disappointed not to find a few shillin's tied up in a stockin'. The cottage were sold, but gran'father bought it hisself, and moved into it with his family; and years passed, and then gran'father, he died of a fever, and gran'mother brought up eleven boys and girls wi' credit. But times got bad, and she were left wi' a cripple daughter, and the t'others scattered away from her, and work failed her, and they were close on comin' to the House. Gran'mother, she had selled most on her furniture, and there were at last but a crust o' bread in the place, and she were makin' tea-kettle broth—for she were Devonshire, and they folk is great at that—when all on a sudden, as she were a-sayin', "Now, Alice, this be our last meal in this dear place," the words of great-gran'mother come surgin' and rushin' through her brain. "Sally, my girl, when you come to want, pull up a yaller marigold by the roots!" and with a hop and a skip, though she were turned seventy-five, she goes straight down the garden, and tugs at a fine yaller marigold. It took a power o' strength to pull it up; and there to the bottom o' the roots was a pot. She pulled of it up, and it were full o' silver and gold, and kept her and her daughter in ease for ever after.'

'Till they went to the grave,' put in Patty solemnly.

'And do you bury your savings?' asked Elfie, laughing.

Deb looked at Patty, and Patty looked at Deb with grave consideration. Then Deb spoke:

'There is things we can't just confide to every one, young ladies. Will you be havin' a taste of Patty's hot cake before you leave? It's just time for it to be comin' out of the oven!'

Patty bustled forward to procure it. Nothing pleased the old women more than to show hospitality to any visitors who came to see them.

While the cake was being got ready, Clare went out to look at the beehives with Deb.

They chatted over them for a few minutes, and then Deb put her hand gently on Clare's arm.

'We've heard o' your sad loss, my dear, and our old hearts have ached for you. 'Tis a heavy cross to have the hope of bein' a happy wife snatched away, and a lone and loveless spinster's lot instead stretchin' out in front o' you. 'Tis a long and weary road for young feet to travel!'

Poor Clare burst into tears. She could not bear, as yet, to be reminded of her trouble.

'Don't talk of it, Deb,' she said between her sobs; 'it only makes it worse.'

'Ay, ay,' said the old woman, wiping a sympathetic tear away from her own eye with the corner of her apron; 'ye'll be feelin' it sore for a time. But the good Lord will comfort you, if no one else will.'

'It is so dreadful to have to live, whether you like it or not,' said Clare, in that little burst of confidence she sometimes showed to strangers, though never to her sisters.

'But seems as if it would not be easier to die if one left the work that has been set us to others to finish,' said Deb gravely.

'I have no work at all,' Clare responded quickly, almost passionately. 'I could have been a good wife—I hope I could—but there's nothing left me now; no one wants me, and there's nothing to do, and I'm sick of everybody and everything!'

'I'm no preacher,' said Deb meditatively, 'and I don't live a saintly life, so it's no good my settin' myself above my fellows, but Patty and me has our Bibles out once every weekday, and most of all Sundays we're readin' it, so I'll make so bold as to pass you a verse that I did a powerful lot of thinkin' over last Sunday. 'Tis this, and maybe, with your quick, eddicated brain, you'll take it in quicker nor I did— "Strengthened with all might, according to His glorious power, unto all patience and longsuffering, with joyfulness." Maybe that's your work just at present, my dear. Shall we go in now?'

Clare's eyes shone through her tears. Slowly and dimly she was seeing light through her darkness. Miss Villars had done much to help her. But nothing seemed to have shown her the grandeur of suffering as this one verse, uttered in slow, halting accents by an uncultured woman. She never forgot it. The verse—God's message to her—was then and there engraved upon her heart; and though she had not yet found her 'rightful resting-place,' though she was still alternately halting and groping her way towards the Light, yet the possibilities of a noble life, a life in the midst of crushing sorrow, such as represented by Deb's text, had a wonderful attraction for her. She was very silent all the way home that afternoon, and shut herself into the study for some hours' more reading; but this time her poems were laid aside, and the Bible had taken their place. It was only a day or two after that she had a great joy.

She received a little parcel from Mrs. Knox, containing a small Testament, a gift of her own to her lover, and inside a letter addressed to her in his handwriting. It had been written just before that fatal day when he had sallied forth so unthinkingly to his death.

'MY DARLING,—

'Just a line to-night, for I may not have much time to write again before the mail. We are off into the bush tomorrow on one of our business expeditions. How I have longed lately for our work to be done, and the steamer to be bringing me back to you! I have been having grave talks lately with one of our fellows who is a religious chap. It has brought vividly before me your sweet gravity in the quaint old study that last night we spent together just before I left, when you told me that you thought we both might have more comfort if we had more religion. Do you remember? What will you say when I tell you that I have found out that you are right? I cannot express myself, darling, as I should wish, but I can tell you that your little Testament is my best friend. I have discovered that religion is something more than a head belief. And here, in the stillness of my tent, I confess—'

This was all. He had evidently broken off hurriedly, and the letter had found its way to Clare to give her its unfinished message of hope. She bowed her head over it in the silence of her room, and then down on her knees she dropped in a burst of thankfulness for the mercy and tenderness shown her in letting her receive such a message. All rebellion and mistrust faded away, and in true humility and penitence Clare was enabled to take the final step towards the realization of that peace she had longed for all her life—that peace that only comes to a soul that has truly sought and found its Saviour.

CHAPTER XIV

THE COUSINS' RETURN

"Tis sweet to hear the watch-dog's honest bark
Bay deep-mouthed welcome as we draw near home;
'Tis sweet to know there is an eye will mark
Our coming, and look brighter when we come.'

—Byron

'Agatha! Clare! I have had an adventure! Where are you? Oh,
here you are; now listen!'

Elfie ran breathlessly into the house one afternoon in great
excitement. She had been for a walk, and had come in late
for tea. Agatha was writing letters at her davenport in the
drawing-room, and Clare was still toying with her cup of tea.
A book was in her lap, but her thoughts were far away. Her
face still wore its sad and somewhat wistful look; yet there
was gradually dawning upon it the sense of repose and rest.
Her sisters noted the old fretfulness and restlessness had
gone out of her tones, and whilst Elfie wondered, Agatha
rejoiced that trouble had not hardened or embittered her.

Elfie threw herself into a seat, looking the picture of health and fresh young beauty.

'I have been to the pine woods,' she began eagerly, 'and I was rejoicing in my solitude, and walking along through the very darkest part, when I heard voices coming towards me. I wondered if it would turn out to be Major Lester and any of his friends, for I knew he had a private gate into the wood from his grounds. So, not wanting to meet any one, I turned down a side path, and then if you please came plump against the very man I wanted to avoid—Major Lester himself. He quite started when he saw me, but took off his hat and tried to be civil. You know I have been introduced to him at the Millers'. I apologised if I were trespassing, and then he said with a little bow, "I do not wish to keep my neighbours at a distance, Miss Dane; you are welcome to use any foot-path through my woods. I have no secrets on my property, I am thankful to say!" I thought that rather nasty of him, for I knew he meant our cupboard, but I murmured something polite, and was just going to turn back, when the voices I had heard came nearer, and suddenly two strange young men came down the path in front of us. You should have seen Major Lester's face; he stared as if he couldn't believe his eyes, and his hand resting on his stick trembled as if he had the palsy. Then he made a step forward,—

"Roger, my boy, is it you, or do my eyes play me false?"

'Before I could get away, one young man said in a most emphatic voice, and rather sternly too, I thought, "I have brought him back to you, uncle, and he will tell you for himself whether my poor father or I had any hand in his disappearance!" Then I made my escape; I heard them all talking at once. Isn't it exciting? The lost ones have come back. I think they had walked from Brambleton station— taken the short cut through the woods. They looked as if they had roughed it. So weather-beaten and worn!'

'This is an excitement,' Agatha said, turning round from her writing; 'what is Alick Lester like, Elfie?'

'Oh, I didn't notice, I hadn't time. They were both tall, broad-shouldered men in rough shooting clothes, I think. Do you think they will be paying us a visit, Agatha?'

'I suppose Mr. Alick Lester will,' and Agatha's face assumed rather an anxious expression, as she remembered her charge.

'Where is he going to live, I wonder?' said Clare; 'it may seem to him that we are usurpers. Do you think he knows about his father's legacy to you, Agatha?'

Agatha shook her head doubtfully.

'I don't know. I suppose his lawyer will have told him, if he has been to see him. I expect he will stay up at the Hall. Major Lester would be hard-hearted indeed if he did not make him welcome after finding his long-lost son!'

The next morning the whole village was in excitement with the news. Miss Miller tore here and there, pulling at her bonnet strings, and quite incoherent in her speech.

'The vicar is asking Alick to put up with us,' she said, meeting Agatha out. 'It is very trying for him, poor fellow, to find both his father and home taken from him, and it's not to be expected that he would stay long at the Hall, and if his father hadn't died, you wouldn't be where you are, and I suppose we did misunderstand him; but if he had come to church regularly he would have found us his friends, and what he will do now I can't think! I can't stop a minute; I must see Major Lester before our quarterly meeting about church expenses, which takes place this afternoon at two o'clock; and I have just remembered that the bed-hangings of the spare room bed are at the laundry, and if Alick is to sleep there to night I must superintend the cleaning of the room myself!'

Agatha smiled as she returned home, and wondered if there was anything in the vicarage or parish that Miss Miller did not superintend.

Early in the afternoon Clare, who was doing a little gardening, was startled by the sudden appearance of Agatha in the greatest distress of mind, and quite shaken out of her usual composure.

'Oh, Clare, whatever shall I do? I have lost a most important little packet, and I am dreadfully afraid it has been stolen from me.'

'What packet?'

'A small packet Mr. Lester gave to me. I did not say anything about it, because he did not wish me to. I put it in my dressing-case, which always stands on my dressing-table, and I placed it in the secret drawer. The drawer is empty, and the paper gone. I was to give it to his son when he returned, and I promised to keep it safely. I cannot imagine what can have become of it! What shall I do? I wonder how any one could have found it. It is a perfect mystery to me!'

'You must have forgotten where you put it,' said Clare; 'let me come and look. It is quite impossible for any one to have stolen it.'

But Clare's search was quite as unsuccessful as Agatha's, and the latter became almost tearful in her agitation and distress.

'Mr. Alick Lester will be sure to call, and it was his father's wish he should open the cupboard. How can he do it, when I have lost the directions?'

'Is that all the packet contained?' asked Clare, looking relieved. 'I had no idea you possessed the key to it! How quiet you have kept it! And now I will surprise you by telling you that I have found out myself the way to open that cupboard, so am quite independent of any written instructions!'

Agatha certainly was surprised, and though thankful when Clare related her experience to her, did not feel more at ease.

'I have been careless of my charge,' she said. 'What will Mr. Alick think of me? And it is alarming to think that some one has got possession of the secret. They may have opened the cupboard already, for all I know, or may be going to do it this very night. I wonder if our maids are to be trusted! Perhaps Jane has been tampering with my case.'

'I am sure she wouldn't. You don't walk in your sleep, do you?'

Agatha gave a little laugh.

'No, you know I do not. I remember looking at it only a week ago, and putting it carefully back again.'

'Was any one in the room when you did it?'

'No—at least Jane came in, I remember, for she startled me, but she would never know what it was.'

There was silence; then Agatha said more slowly, 'It does look rather suspicious, now I have remembered about Jane, because she has been such friends lately with Major Lester's valet. You know she always walks home from church with him. Elfie was laughing about it, and saying she had soon picked up a follower.'

'I don't see the connection between those two threads,' said Clare, 'unless you think Major Lester is a thief himself!'

'I don't know what I think,' said Agatha hopelessly, sitting down on a chair, and looking the picture of woe; 'I only know I have lost what I promised to keep safely, and I know that Major Lester's great desire has been to get at that cupboard. We won't say anything about it to the maids, Clare, but I will write a little note to Mr. Alick, asking him to come and see me the first thing to-morrow morning. I will tell him exactly what has happened, and then with your help he can open the cupboard, and we shall no longer have the responsibility of it.'

With this wise decision Agatha brightened up, and Clare, who loved nothing better than a mystery, grew quite animated in discussing the matter, and offering her advice. Elfie was taken into counsel, and the three resolved to say nothing till they laid the facts before Alick Lester.

One of the maids was despatched with a note to the Hall, and Agatha received a polite reply from the young man, saying that he hoped to call on her about eleven o'clock the next morning.

But Agatha could get no sleep that night; she was anxious and ill at ease, and after tossing about in bed, long after the rest of the household were deep in sleep, she rose to pace her room, as she sometimes did when wakeful.

Her lips were moving in prayer, and she was endeavouring, as was her custom, to commit her trouble to One above,

Amy Le Feuvre

when she was distinctly conscious of stealthy footsteps treading the gravel path below her window. It was a bright moonlight night, and she had no light burning. For one moment she hesitated; then quietly she walked to the window, which was partly open, and cautiously moving the blind looked out.

The shadow of a man turning the corner of the house towards the study window met her gaze, and Agatha realized that the time had come for immediate action. She was naturally a brave woman; yet for an instant, when she remembered they were but a houseful of women, her courage faltered. Only for an instant. Her motto, 'Trust in the Lord,' flashed like a light across her path, and throwing on her dressing gown, she left her room with quiet, steady steps. She roused Clare, who slept in the next room, and who, full of nerves and fancies as she was, delighted in any nocturnal adventure.

'We really ought to have revolvers,' she said, as she rapidly prepared to follow Agatha downstairs. 'What have you got in your hand? A poker?'

'Don't make a noise; I think we shall frighten any one away without rousing the whole house.'

Clare valiantly seized both poker and tongs in her room, and crept downstairs. Agatha led the way, a candle in hand. They reached the study, and Agatha threw open the door. To her horror the French window was wide open, and a man was on his knees by the cupboard, a lantern on the ground. He started to his feet; then, bewildered and utterly unprepared for their sudden intrusion, dashed out on the verandah and disappeared, but not before both Agatha and Clare had plainly recognised him. He was Major Lester's valet!

Agatha hastily closed the window and shutters, then looked

at Clare, who was now white and trembling.

'This looks bad, Clare,' she said gravely. 'This window and shutters must have been purposely left unfastened. He could never have unfastened them from outside.'

But now the danger was over Clare's courage had vanished. She grasped hold of Agatha's arm.

'Come upstairs, quick! He may come back and murder us! I won't stay downstairs another minute.'

'There is nothing to fear now. He has gone. I don't think he would dare face us after being recognised. Wait a minute. Look! He has left an envelope lying by his lantern, and I believe—yes, it is mine. And in Mr. Lester's handwriting. Jane must be at the bottom of this!'

'Come upstairs. I won't stay down here a minute longer!'

And Clare fled trembling to her room. Agatha did not go up till she had made sure the windows and shutters were securely fastened, and had also been the round of the house. Then she went to Clare, who was in such a panic of fright that she persuaded her to come and share her bed; and after she had grown calmer and finally dropped asleep, Agatha lay quiet and sleepless, revolving the events of the night, and praying for wisdom in dealing with the suspected Jane.

The next morning, immediately after breakfast, she called her into her room, and the very sight of her white trembling face proved her guilt. By dint of cross questioning, and much entreaty, Agatha was at last possessed of all information.

Watson, Major Lester's valet, was a devoted admirer of Jane. Together they often talked over their respective master and mistress, and Watson had told her of Major Lester's unsatisfactory interview with Agatha.

'It's some family papers that is locked up in that there cupboard he is wild to get at, and he says he has a right to 'em; and so he has, for he told a gentleman who was visitin' him that they would do him a mischief if they got into wrong hands. And it seems that Mr. Tom told Miss Dane all about 'em, and gave her the secret of opening that cupboard.'

From this statement Watson went on to work upon Jane's love of discovering a mystery and her insatiable curiosity; and at last led her to thoroughly search Agatha's room for any papers bearing on the subject. Quite by accident she came upon the secret drawer in the dressing-case. The fastening had become insecure, and, trembling at her audacity, Jane carried the packet to her lover, begging him to return it to her when he had possessed himself of its secret. The next move was to get her to leave the study windows unfastened, and here Jane's fortitude gave way.

'I know it was wicked, ma'am, but Watson, he told me it couldn't do you a injury; he wasn't a housebreaker, he wouldn't lay his finger on any property of yours! he only wanted to get his master what rightfully belonged to him. Major Lester, he would handsomely reward him for it, and so I did as he told me, but I never slept a wink all last night, and when I heard you go downstairs, I could have screamed out "Murder!" I was that scared.'

Then Jane begged and prayed with heartfelt sobs for forgiveness, and Agatha, feeling a pity for her, told her she would not dismiss her without a character, as at first she had determined to do, but would let her stay on for the month, at the end of which time she must go, as she could never keep a maid who had proved so utterly untrustworthy.

Coming downstairs from this interview with a worn face and anxious heart, Agatha was met by Elfie.

'Mr. Lester has come, Agatha. I met him in the garden, and he is in the drawing-room waiting for you.'

CHAPTER XV

ALICK LESTER

He was a man of honour, of noble and generous nature.'

—Longfellow

Mr. Alick Lester proved to be a pleasant, frank young fellow, with the sunniest eyes and smile that Agatha had ever seen. She took to him at once, and found herself telling him without any hesitation the history of the lost packet. He listened attentively, but was indignant when Agatha hinted that Watson might have acted under the major's instructions.

'No, Miss Dane, my uncle is a gentleman. He would never stoop so low as that. I know he tried to blacken my dear father's character, but he idolized his son, and hardly realized the mischief he was doing. Watson is a thorough scoundrel! I have always known it, and my uncle has already dismissed him for tampering with some of his letters. He was telling us about it last night, and Watson leaves him at the end of this week. Depend upon it, the chap was trying to get the papers in his own hands for ends of his own, and I think you were awfully plucky to catch him at it as you did. But now we must get hold of him at once, and get the packet from him.'

'I expect he will have left the neighbourhood,' said Agatha. 'If you wish to open the cupboard, my sister will tell you the secret. She has accidentally discovered it. Shall we go to the study now?'

The young man agreed at once to this proposal, and when Clare came forward, he looked at her with secret laughter in his eyes.

'They say a woman never rests content under a mystery,' he said; 'and you have proved my good angel, so I can only avow my gratitude. But do you know that from a boy I have viewed that cupboard as impenetrable as the sphinx itself? And yet my energy or ambition to solve its secret was never sufficient to allow me to succeed. My father always told me that age had some advantages, and that when the time came for me to know all that he did, I should do so.'

Clare flushed and felt very uncomfortable; then she met the young man's gaze calmly.

'I know I have shown the weakness of our sex, but it is not often one is brought into contact with such a mystery; and having had your father's Arabic motto translated to me, I could not resist the temptation of trying to prove its truth. I need not say I have not opened the cupboard. That temptation I was enabled to resist.'

'And the motto?' inquired the young man, passing his hand almost tenderly over his father's handiwork, and a shade coming over his brow as he spoke.

Clare's face was sad too, as she remembered from whom the translation had come, but she repeated quietly,—

   "A closed bud containeth

Amy Le Feuvre

Possibilities infinite and unknown."

Then, stooping down, she turned the carved bud, until a sharp click was heard, and the door moved forwards; and then linking her arm in that of Agatha the sisters left the room, and Alick Lester was alone with the secret solved at last.

Two or three hours passed, and still he was shut in the study. When he at last appeared in the drawing-room, he seemed to have left his youth and brightness behind him there. He asked with knitted brow and anxious face if he might speak to Agatha alone, and then drawing a dusty leather portfolio from under his arm he held it out to her, saying, 'I received a letter written by my father shortly before his death, and which he had left in the charge of our lawyer. He told me to give this to you. I fancy it may not prove so valuable to you as my dear father hoped. It is merely a collection of notes of his, and a few valuable papers about some Assyrian and Egyptian antiquities. He always hoped to write a book upon the subject, but put off doing so until he could obtain more information on certain points, or links, that were missing.'

Agatha took her legacy very calmly.

'I daresay my sister Gwen, who is now abroad, will be interested in it. She is very fond of antiquities of all sorts.'

Then looking at the young fellow's dazed, troubled face, she said sympathetically, 'I am afraid you have spent a sad morning in looking over your father's belongings.'

He laughed a little shortly.

'I have had a shock, and feel bewildered. I have not the faintest idea how to act, and it is at present all dark to me.

Miss Dane, you are a good woman, my father says. Will you pray that I may have right guidance about a very difficult matter? And may I come and see you again? I shall be staying at the Crown Hotel in Brambleton for the present. The Millers wanted me to go to them, but I cannot. If I stayed in this village at all, it would have to be at the Hall, and they—I do not want that.'

'I hope you do not look upon us as usurpers,' said Agatha. 'I cannot tell you how guilty I feel sometimes about accepting this house from your father, especially since your return. It seems as if you ought to be here.'

Then Alick Lester looked up with his sunny smile.

'Miss Dane, I assure you I would never live here! My future is to be spent either out in the colonies or—or in a different house to this. And I cannot tell you what a cheery, home-like aspect you have given to this old house. I am sure you are a boon to the neighbourhood, and I should like, if you don't think it forward of me upon so short an acquaintance, to look upon you all as friends.'

He grasped her hand warmly and departed; and from that time forward he was on a friendly and familiar footing with the inmates of his old home.

Watson was found to have already left the neighbourhood, as Agatha surmised, and no one was able to trace his movements. Not wishing to create disturbance in the village, Agatha did not mention his nocturnal visit to any one, and Alick was the only one who knew of it besides themselves. Elfie and Clare were both rather disappointed that the mystery of the cupboard seemed to be such a common-place affair, but they noticed that it had brought a great deal of anxious thought to Alick Lester. His face was almost

Amy Le Feuvre

careworn at times, and he seemed now to spend most of his time in London, occasionally coming to have a further rummage in the cupboard.

'It is crammed full of old letters and papers,' he said once to Agatha; 'and if you will let me look through them on the spot, it will be such a help to me.'

One day he brought in Roger Lester, and introduced him; and after that the two young fellows often dropped in to afternoon tea, assuring Agatha that they never felt so much at home anywhere else. They both had a fund of high spirits, and though Alick at times looked absorbed and pre-occupied in anxious thought, he knew how to throw it aside and be as light-hearted as his cousin.

They were sitting one afternoon on the verandah outside the drawing-room, when Roger turned to Agatha and remarked,—

'You would not imagine it, Miss Dane, but we two have grown up with such perfect *cameraderie* that until quite lately, I believe, we have never concealed a single thing from each other. And now if you hear of us drifting apart, and our liking turning to hate, you will know the cause—it is the renowned old carved cupboard.'

Alick had been talking and laughing with Elfie, but he stopped instantly as if he had been shot when he heard this speech, and there was an awkward silence for a minute.

Roger added with a laugh, 'It is some skeleton he has unearthed; but why he should refuse to let me share in the secret I can't imagine!'

'I don't think we need make it a matter of public talk,' said Alick hotly.

His cousin looked at him in astonishment, then changed the subject with a shrug of his shoulders and a laugh.

When they were gone Clare said thoughtfully, 'There is a mystery after all, and not a very pleasant one, apparently. I feel sorry for Mr. Alick.'

'Which do you like the best of the cousins?' asked Elfie carelessly.

Clare's face looked sad as she replied, 'Oh, I don't know. I don't think any young man is worth a thought. They amuse one by their fun, but I would just as soon not have them come here so often. Miss Miller will be attacking us soon on the subject. She was beginning this morning, when I met her out, but I always flee from her when she is in her aggressive moods.'

'What did she say?'

Clare looked at her younger sister with a little smile.

'Perhaps I had better not tell you. She saw you cut a rose off the other afternoon and offer it to Mr. Alick, and she considers that the depth of iniquity. "Such a piece of audacious flirting I have rarely seen carried on within a few yards from an open road in full view of any passer-by!" And then she turned the tables on me, and I came off, because she was making me boil with indignation. I think she delights in making her fellow-creatures as uncomfortable as possible.'

'It is only her way,' put in Agatha; 'she does not realize what a sting her words have. She told me last Sunday, when I unfortunately gave an order to some of my Sunday class in front of her, that however much I might try to slight her and usurp her place in the vicarage and parish I would not be

Amy Le Feuvre

successful, for the vicar was proof against all young ladies' blandishments!'

'She ought to be horsewhipped!' cried Elfie hotly, and then she began to laugh.

'There is one that is a match for her in the parish, and that is Deb Howitt. She was covering a chair at the vicarage, and Miss Miller was abusing some of the congregation—I forget who it was now. It was about the behaviour of some girls—I think she is always specially hard on them—and Deb looked at her very quietly. "Ay, ma'am, we mustn't grudge them their sweethearts! 'Tis better for most to have the cares of a family to soften them, for 'tis the spinsters that have the name for getting hard and bitter. Sharp tongues are not so frequent amongst mothers, and the world would be better without bitterness, I reckon!" Miss Miller shut up at once.'

'Deb asked me yesterday when Gwen was coming back. What do you think, Agatha?' said Clare.

'I don't know at all. You know what her last letter said. That Walter had sold his farm and gone off with Mr. Montmorency, and she was staying with Mrs. Montmorency in Loreto. She did not seem in a hurry to leave, and as long as she is happy we must be content that she should be out there.'

And the autumn came and went, and winter set in without any word or sign from Gwen of home-coming.

Alick and Roger spent the autumn in Scotland, but Christmas found them both at the Hall. Major Lester seemed to have overcome his dislike to his nephew, and the Hall was quite a cheerful centre in the village. Visitors came and went, and Agatha and her sisters were asked up there more frequently than they cared to go.

Agatha still possessed Alick's confidence. He would come to her for advice, as most people did, but yet would never touch upon his serious difficulty; and she sometimes wondered if the cupboard's secret was no longer a trouble to him.

'Do you think I am leading a lazy life?' he asked her one day, when he met her walking out and insisted upon accompanying her home.

'I think you are. It is always a pity when young men have enough income to live independently without any responsibility attaching to their wealth.'

'I am not wealthy,' he responded quickly. 'I have just enough to live upon. What do you think of Roger? He is as idle as I at present.'

'I think not. He helps his father with the property, which is a large one, and if anything happened to Major Lester he would have his hands full.'

Alick laughed a little hardly.

'Lucky fellow! So if I were in his shoes you would not find fault with me!'

'I think,' said Agatha gently, 'that each one of us ought to realize that we are not placed in this world to live for ourselves. There is so much to do for others who need our help. You are young now, and have life stretching out in front of you. Do not waste it, do not have to acknowledge when your life is over that no one will have been the better for your existence.'

Amy Le Feuvre

'Would you have one sink one's own individuality in the lives of others, like some of our great philanthropists?'

'No, our first duty is to ourselves. I think too many in the present day rush into work of all sorts, trying to please and satisfy others at the expense of their own peace and satisfaction, and that is wrong.'

'I don't understand you.'

'I mean this. We have two lives: the outer one which every one sees, and the inner one which only God and ourselves know about. Our inner life is the more important one of the two, is it not? For it is the spiritual part of us that is immortal. First let us satisfy and ensure the safety of our own souls, before we seek to satisfy the hungry and thirsty ones around us. And then if our inner life is adjusted rightly—is in touch (shall I say?) with its Maker—the helping others becomes a pleasure as well as a necessity.'

Alick did not reply, and Agatha delicately turned the subject; but her words made him ponder much afterwards, and had far more effect upon him than ever she imagined.

CHAPTER XVI

BRINGING BAD TIDINGS

'A man should never be ashamed to own he has been in the wrong, which is but saying, in other words, that he is wiser to-day than he was yesterday.'

—Pope

It was towards the end of February that old Nannie sat by her fire in the peaceful almshouse in which she had taken shelter. Rain was falling fast, and when she heard a knock at her door, she hardly turned in her chair, for she thought it could be only one of her neighbours come for a chat.

When the new-comer came silently forward and stood in front of her, Nannie looked up with a gasp and a cry.

'Miss Gwen! My dear Miss Gwen, is it you? Where do you come from? And oh, how ill you look!'

Gwen bent over the old woman and kissed her; then she took a seat by her and gave a hard little laugh.

'Oh no, I am not ill. I wish I could be—at least, I am almost coward enough to wish it. I only landed early this morning in

Amy Le Feuvre

the London Docks. I have come from California, Nannie. Aren't you glad to see me?'

Gwen was clad in a plain dark blue serge and sailor hat, but somehow had not her habitual neat appearance. Her face was wan and white, she seemed to have aged ten years, and her once sparkling eyes were now dim and worn-looking.

'Just off a voyage,' murmured Nannie, putting on her spectacles and peering anxiously into her face. 'Ay, my dear, surely them foreign parts don't bring such change and misery to all the folks who venture out?'

Gwen laughed again.

'Every one, I hope, has not had my experience,' she said. 'If I may quote from your favourite book, Nannie, I can say truly, "I went out full, and have been brought home again empty!"'

'"The Lord hath brought me home again empty,"' corrected Nannie.

Then Gwen leant forward, and taking Nannie's two hands in hers, she said in a hard, strained voice:

'Nannie, I have come to you because I am desperate, and I thought perhaps you would give me courage to face them at home. I have never had such a hard task set me in my life; but I deserve it, and I am not going to flinch from my duty. I have ruined four people's lives, my own included!'

She strangled a dry sob in her throat, then went on,— grasping the withered hands in hers, as a drowning man might a rope,—'Nannie, do you remember my verse you gave me this time last year?'

'Ay, Miss Gwen, my dear, surely, and many's the prayer I've offered up at the throne of grace for you! "Commit thy way unto the Lord, trust also in Him, and He shall bring it to pass!" Maybe you've come to the end of your own ways by this time—will that be it?'

'Judgment has come on me. I was so sure, so certain of my plans. I frustrated every difficulty, I forced some against their will to assist me in carrying them out; and yet all this last year your verse has haunted me. I was determined to be independent of God. I was so self-assured, and my pride and spirit carried me through all, that I laughed at the idea of failure; and then when the blow fell, it crushed every atom of self-confidence and spirit out of me! I am a poor, miserable, broken-down creature, Nannie; what can you say to help me?'

Nannie gently withdrew her hands, and leaning forward, placed them on Gwen's shoulders. Then in a tender, solemn tone she said, '"Blessed are the poor in spirit, for theirs is the kingdom of heaven!"'

There was dead silence for a few moments, and then Gwen bowed her head in her old nurse's lap, and tears came thick and fast.

Nannie let her cry on, but her lips moved in prayer. 'Dear Lord, Thou hast smitten to heal; Thou hast broken to mend; let her meet with Thee now, and get Thy blessing!'

'I have never shed a tear until now,' uttered Gwen at last, looking up at Nannie with almost a pathetic look in her tear-dimmed eyes. 'I felt my trouble was too great for tears. I was turning to stone until I saw you. Oh, Nannie, if you knew all, you would be sorry for me!'

Will you be telling it to me, Miss Gwen?'

'Yes, indeed I will.'

Gwen gave a rough sketch of her life for the first month with her brother. She told of the bitter blow it was to find him about to be married; and then told Nannie of Mr. Montmorency's arrival, and the pressure put upon her brother to sell his farm, and join him in his quest for gold.

'I gave him no rest, Nannie, until he promised to do as I wanted. I even went to the girl he was going to marry, and coaxed and entreated her to add her persuasions to mine. She was bitterly disappointed, poor little thing, at their marriage being postponed, but she was thoroughly unselfish, and only thought of Walter's good. Mr. Montmorency worked hard too. He wanted more capital, and said Walter must do his share in getting it, if he was to be a partner, so I worked with all my might and main to get it for him. I persuaded Meta Seton to invest a legacy of hers in the scheme; I wrote home and implored all the others to invest in it too. I put all the money I had myself in it, and then when all was done, and I had broken up Walter's home, I sat down in complacency and waited for the success that was sure to follow. I can't tell you when the first doubts of the whole thing crept into my mind. I only know the last four months have been ones of torturing suspense and uncertainty. I wonder I have not come home grey-headed. The crash came six weeks or so ago. Mr. Montmorency, after ruining himself, my brother, and hundreds of others, decamped, and has not been heard of since. It was simply a mad speculation set on foot by a clever man with little capital of his own. Walter is ruined; he has crept back to his own part of the country, and has to begin life all over again; his hopes of a married life and a happy home have been dashed to the ground. Meta's father is so enraged at his daughter's legacy being lost, that he has forbidden Walter the house, and his bride as well as his farm has been taken from him. I wonder he did not curse me, as he came to see me off in the steamer; but his face—the hopelessness and despair written there—was quite enough for me. And now I am going back to break to Clare and Elfie that they as well as myself are absolute beggars. Agatha was the only wise one amongst us. She refused to trust Mr. Montmorency with one farthing of her money.'

'Ay, my dear, it's terrible—terrible for you; but loss of money is not ruin. You have health and strength and youth to sustain you, and though the cloud has been dark, it will have a silver lining!'

'How can I tell them!' cried Gwen; and her face grew set and hard, as she stood up, and dashed the tear-drops from her eyelashes. 'They have no idea I am returning home, or what has happened. I have been to our lawyer before I came to you, and though he has heard bad reports of Mr. Montmorency, he has never said a word to them. Do you realize I have beggared our whole family, Nannie? Poor Clare has had trouble enough of her own, without this in addition; and Elfie, who has never had a care or thought, how will she take it? I wish—I wish I were dead!'

'Hush, hush, my dear!' said Nannie, almost sternly. 'That would be a coward's wish, and you are not that! If you learn the lesson the Lord would have you learn, you may yet live to find that this big trouble has been the biggest blessing in your life.'

'Do you think if I had been like Agatha, who prays even if she goes shopping that she may spend the money properly, and if I had committed my plans to God, this would have happened, Nannie?'

'No, I don't think it would,' was Nannie's grave reply.

Then there was silence, which Nannie broke by begging Gwen to have some refreshment.

'No, thank you, Nannie, I must be going. I wish I had done with life, and was in an almshouse with you. It would be so easy to be all that one ought to be. Good-bye, you old dear. Pray for me, for I have a dreadful time before me, and I don't see how on earth we are to live. I shall have to earn money somehow at once. Perhaps I shall go into service—that is the fashion now. Ladies are becoming servants to the class who used to be in service. Give me your blessing and let me go!'

Gwen was talking fast and lightly to hide her emotion, but old Nannie took hold of her hands and looked up at her very solemnly.

'My dear Miss Gwen, you have heard God's voice speaking to you many times since you were a little girl. You are hearing it again now. Are you going to close your ear to it? If your pride and self-confidence is crumbled to dust, 'tis the opportunity to confess it to Him who hates a proud look, and says the humble shall be exalted. Take your bitterness of soul to the Saviour, and He will heal and comfort you. Promise me you will listen to His voice!'

'You're a saint, Nannie; I promise you I will pray, if I have never done so before. Good-bye.'

She went out into the pouring rain, found her way back to the station, and an hour after was at Waterloo Station starting for Brambleton. She was just getting into the carriage when some one accosted her. It was Clement Arkwright, who had travelled out to California with her. He looked unfeignedly pleased to see her.

'Just come home again, Miss Dane? How did you like California?'

Gwen hardly knew how to answer him. A rush of memories came over her. The time on board ship when she had so systematically avoided him, and cultivated with assiduity the one who had ruined her, stood up before her with awful distinctness. But she pulled herself together, and tried to speak unconcernedly.

'I am glad to be back again.'

'How is your brother? I hope the report I heard was not true, that he had joined Alf Montmorency in his search for gold?'

Gwen was in the carriage now, and the train was just starting. She spoke on the impulse of the moment, and Clement Arkwright never forgot the look of despairing hopelessness on her face as she held out her hand to him.

'Good-bye—we are off. You told me once that I would bring disaster upon myself by my obstinate wilfulness. I have done so. You warned me on the steamer against Mr. Mont-morency. But I would not listen, and he has ruined the whole lot of us.'

The train steamed out of the station, and Clement Arkwright turned away with a grave, thoughtful face.

'Poor Gwen! Yet it will be the making of her, if she can once be got to confess that her judgment is not infallible. I should like to get hold of that scoundrel!'

It was about five o'clock when Gwen reached Brambleton. She left her luggage at the station, and tramped through the driving rain and wind with fierce indifference, arriving at

Amy Le Feuvre

Jasmine Cottage with drenched garments, and weary, foot-sore feet.

The lamps were lighted in the drawing-room, and the shutters were not closed. Gwen stepped quietly up to the window and looked in. It was a cosy, cheerful scene. Agatha was sitting with a smile on her face by a bright fire, knitting in hand. Clare was reading aloud on the opposite side of the fireplace, and Elfie in her favourite position on the low fender-stool, tempting a grey Persian kitten to perform acrobatical antics with Agatha's ball of wool.

'How changed will be the scene a few minutes later!' thought Gwen bitterly, and she knocked sharply at the door. It was opened by a maid who had superseded Jane, and who looked suspiciously at the drenched figure.

'You have mistaken this for the vicarage,' she said super-ciliously. 'If you want shelter or food, you will get it there!'

Gwen swung her aside with a quick impatient laugh, and opened the drawing-room door. In another moment, with cries of astonishment and delight, her sisters were caressing and welcoming her; but she pushed them away from her.

'Let me tell you how I come back first,' she said sharply. 'You will not give me such a hearty welcome when you know. I have ruined Walter; the gold company has been a big swindle, and every penny of our money has all gone. Now what do you say to me?'

'Never mind the money now,' said Agatha, who was never discomposed. 'Come upstairs to bed at once, you are wet through. How could you walk through such a storm! Not another word till you have had something to eat. Come along —you are dead beat.'

She led her away, motioning to Clare and Elfie not to follow, and they stood looking at each other with dazed, bewildered eyes.

'Does she mean it? Is it really true?' exclaimed Elfie, 'Oh, how ill she looks!'

'What a dreadful thing for Walter!' was Clare's response; and then the full force of Gwen's words dawned upon them.

'Whatever shall we do? Agatha's hundred pounds will not keep four of us!'

When Agatha returned to the room, nearly an hour later, she found an anxious consultation going on by the fire. Her face was just as placid as usual, though a shade graver.

'I have left her to sleep,' she said; 'it is the best thing for her. She seems quite worn out, and I think it is best for none of us to go near her till the morning.'

'Is it really true what she says?'

'I am afraid so. I would not let her give me details. She is so filled with remorse at having persuaded you to invest your money so, that I saw she was working herself into a perfect fever over it, and I stopped her at once. I am thankful she is home again. I have been very uneasy about her lately.'

'I never thought you were uneasy about anything,' said Clare, trying to smile.

'We are planning what we can do to earn our livelihood, Agatha,' said Elfie. 'Have you any idea to give us?'

'We will not go into that to-night,' was Agatha's quiet

Amy Le Feuvre

response. 'This house is our own, and so is the furniture. We have sufficient for the present. When Gwen has got over the fatigue of her journey, we will have a talk together about ways and means.'

Just before going to her own room for the night, Agatha stepped quietly into Gwen's room.

She found her lying wide awake staring at the flickering fire with a hard set face, and determined lips. Agatha came up and put her hand on her forehead.

'You are feverish,' she said. 'Are you comfortable? Do you not feel sleepy?'

'Would you?' was the quick retort.

'I am sure I should, after the journey you have had. Oh, Gwen dear, don't look so! There are worse losses than money. Don't reproach yourself too much.' And Agatha was so touched by the hopeless misery in her sister's face that tears filled her eyes.

Gwen looked at her, and her face began to soften.

'You're a good old thing, Agatha. I wish I were more like you. You will need all your faith and prayer now, and so will the others. Good-night.'

She turned her face away, and with a kiss and an unspoken prayer, Agatha left her.

CHAPTER XVII

ELFIE'S CHOICE

'Go, whate'er the lot may be
That my Father sends to me,
Never am I comfortless
With His Word to aid and bless;
And while He His help is bringing,
I will cheer the way with singing.'

—Farningham

Gwen refused to have her breakfast in bed the next morning, and appeared downstairs at the usual hour with a white determined face.

She looked in astonishment at Elfie, who was flitting round the room singing merrily, as she added fresh flowers to the vases on the breakfast table.

'Well,' said Elfie, a little defiantly, 'I am not going to be miserable, even if we have lost our money. There is no death in the house, and they say beggars have lighter hearts than kings!'

And she would not have breakfast a silent meal, but chatted

Amy Le Feuvre

and laughed, and had so much to tell Gwen of all that had happened during her absence, that she infected the others with her light-hearted gaiety.

It was after Agatha had done her housekeeping that, sitting round the fire, Gwen gave them full details of all they wished to know. She did not spare herself, and her sisters wondered at the change in her, for never before in their lives had they known Gwen to own herself in the wrong. Then ways and means were discussed, Agatha declared she would send away the two maids at once, and then with the help of a woman from the village, she was sure they could still live together on her income; but this the others would not hear of.

'I would set up a village shop if I had capital,' asserted Gwen, with a little of her old spirit; 'the *role* of governess for needy women is past and gone; but for myself I know I shall not do better than stick to literature. I can write, and I have had many openings which I have refused, because I did not want the grind of it. If I set to work in earnest now, I shall soon bring some grist to the mill.'

'By the bye,' said Agatha, 'I wonder if you could make anything of a fat bundle of manuscripts that Mr. Lester bequeathed to me. I know you love any ancient papers, and though they're Latin and Greek to me, you may make something of them.'

She left the room, and soon returned with the papers. Gwen's eyes glistened as she looked them through. And she seemed to forget time and surroundings as she sat down and pored over them with eager interest.

At last she looked up.

Agatha, if I can put these together, it will prove a valuable legacy. Will you hand them over to me? There will be months' work, but it will be well worth the labour. I know some men in London would give you hundreds of pounds for some of these papers, but I shall not let them slip out of my hands.'

'I am so glad you will be able to make something of them,' responded Agatha simply. 'He said I might make what use I liked of them, so I willingly give them to you.'

'So Gwen's livelihood is secured,' said Clare, trying to speak lightly. 'Now let me tell you what I propose to do. The other day Miss Villars asked me if I knew of any lady who would undertake the post of matron to a small Convalescent Home for clergymen's wives and daughters. It is a private one that Miss Villars has started herself. She said she wanted some one who was quite a lady, and who would be able to make every one feel comfortable and at home. The salary would be about 50 pounds. She said she would only give the post to some one who was really needing the money. I believe she would give it to me at once if I told her how things were with us, and I should like it. I mean to go over to her this afternoon and ask her about it. Well, Agatha, don't you approve? Do you think me too incapable for the house-keeping?'

Clare finished her proposal rather wistfully, and Gwen looked at her in wonder. She had noticed, as perhaps the others had not, the great change that had passed over the wilful, capricious girl during the last six months. There was a subdued tone in her voice, but a glad light in her eye and a quiet restfulness about her manner that had been utterly foreign to her before.

Clare had come through the refining fire, softened and purified; she was a little quieter than she used to be, but every now and then her old, clear laugh would ring out, and if her moods were not so mirthful as Elfie's, they were quite as bright. Quietly and unassumingly she had slipped into the way of giving her help whenever it was needed, and now when Agatha contemplated the possibility of a coming separation from her, she began to realize how much she would miss her. The conversation continued, and then Elfie put in her word.

'And now what in the world am I to do? Will you agree to letting me go up to London and play to the public? I could get pushed on by Professor S——. He told me in Germany he could give me several very good introductions, if I wished to make music my profession. There is really nothing else I am good at.'

No one would hear of this suggestion, and later in the day Agatha confided to Gwen a little of her anxiety about Alick Lester and Elfie.

'I do not think it is fancy. He is a great deal here—more than I like—and now he has no eyes or ears for any one but her. I do not know whether she likes him; I notice she is self-conscious and absorbed when he is here, and that is not at all natural to her.'

'What prospects has he?' asked Gwen abruptly.

'I don't know. I sometimes wish I knew a little more about him. Ever since he has opened the cupboard, he has had something weighing on his mind, and though he tells me he has only about 200 pounds a year to live upon, he seems in no hurry to get anything to do. It is an idle life for him in this small village. He is with his cousin most of his time, but he drops in to see us in the evening; in fact, they both come here a great deal, and though Miss Miller has put her veto on it, nothing will keep them away.'

'I wish Elfie would marry. She is not fit to fight life's battle;' and Gwen sighed as she spoke, and her face relapsed into its now habitual gloom.

But the next day brought a letter that decided Elfie's fate.

She opened it with a grimace at the handwriting.

'Now what does Cousin James want to say to me! Do you think he has heard of our misfortunes?'

She read on, and her face grew thoughtful. Instead of handing it over to any of her sisters to read, she left the room with it in her hand.

And in the privacy of her own bedroom she spread it out before her, and a hard and sore battle commenced in her heart.

The letter was as follows:—

'DEAR ELFRIDA,—

'I have just heard in the city from Watkins, that your clever sister has squandered out in California, all the money that was left you by our aunt. It is a pity that you are all so wilful and ignorant about money matters. However, I am quite willing to come forward and offer my help, though in these hard times, with such an establishment as Dane Hall to keep up, I find it increasingly difficult to live within my income. Your cousin Helen is in very delicate health, and has for some time past felt unequal to managing our large household. She needs some bright companionship; and I now offer you a home with us, on condition that you make yourself generally useful, and relieve your cousin of all the house-keeping details that fret and annoy her. I shall allow you a handsome allowance for dress in addition, as I shall wish to see you suitably dressed for our position here. Let me hear how soon you can come, and I will arrange that you shall be met at the station. Tell Agatha I commend her for her prudence in refusing to let her money be used for speculation. I hope it will be a lesson to Gwendoline in the future. Her self-confidence needed to be shaken.

'Your affectionate cousin,
'JAMES DANE.'

Elfie read and re-read this through in a mist of tears.

'O God,' she murmured, 'anything but this! I cannot go. It would be slow torture! Do Thou guide and direct me, and help me to decide; but oh, if it is possible, do Thou open another door for me!'

Poor Elfie knew well enough that if she asked her sisters' advice, they would be all agreed as to the impossibility of her accepting her cousin's offer. She knew her Cousin Helen would not make her house a happy or an easy home to live in, for she was a weak, nervously-strung woman, with an irritable temper and an abject fear of her husband, whose will was absolute law. And in the secret depths of Elfie's heart there was a strong disinclination, even though she would not own it to herself, to leave home at present. Though Alick Lester had not said much to her, she knew well enough what his state of feelings were about her; his frequent visits were becoming very pleasant to her, and to leave it all, and perhaps never see him again, was hard to contemplate calmly. He often talked to her of going abroad, and she feared he might do so at once, were she gone. Yet, as she looked the matter straight in the face, she could not but acknowledge to herself that she had no right to refuse it.

'I will not live on Agatha's money; she would share her last crust with any of us, but I am young and strong, and this has come when I am looking out for employment. Many a girl would be thankful to have such a home offered her. I must go and do my best, and I must decide myself, without listening to the others. But oh, it will be a hard life after our happy little home together here!'

The battle was won after she had knelt in prayer, and when she joined her sisters again she was her sunny self.

But when she let them read the letter, they were all indignant at the thought of it.

'I should think you would rather sweep a crossing than go!'

'To be a dependent on Cousin James, and a member of his household, would be more than flesh and blood could stand!'

'Can you imagine the life of Cousin Helen's companion?'

And so on, until throwing back her little head importantly, Elfie was able to protest.

'I know you won't approve of it, but I have decided that I shall go, and you must look at the advantages and make the best of it if you want to help me.'

'You shall never go with my consent,' said Agatha, roused from her usual placidity.

'Then,' said Elfie, laughing, 'I shall go without it, or rather, I shall never rest till I have coaxed a consent out of you. Think

Amy Le Feuvre

of living in the dear old place we all love so well, in the lap of luxury, with nothing to do but dress well, and eat well, and order the dinners, and see that the servants do their work properly! And hasn't it just come at the right time, when my future was so unsettled? Now if Clare succeeds in her plan we shall be all provided for, and life will go smoothly again. And we must comfort ourselves with the thought that we are only paying visits away from home, and perhaps next Christmas we may get together again!'

She rattled on, and then ran out of the room to hide the little choke in her throat, and her sisters looked at each other in bewilderment.

'I never could have thought Elfie would have entertained the idea for a minute,' said Agatha; 'she cannot have the same feelings we have about Cousin James if she can so calmly accept his offer. But she was away in Germany, I remember, when it all happened. I suppose it is rather attractive to her than otherwise. She does not know Cousin Helen as we do.'

'She has no proper pride,' said Gwen, with flashing eyes; and then she pulled herself up.

'Well, I have driven her to it. That will be consolation to me!'

'She talks very lightly of leaving home,' said Clare. 'I wish I had her happy way of looking at things. Nothing seems to trouble her.'

It needed a great deal of coaxing and persuasion to bring her sisters round to her way of thinking; but Elfie was allowed at last to send off her letter accepting her cousin's offer, and none of them ever knew how much it cost her to do it.

Her sunny temper and light-hearted mirth often hid a good

deal of feeling; but, like many others with such a disposition, she never got the credit of taking life seriously.

'She is such a child,' Agatha would say; 'she will be happy in any circumstances. I am thankful she does not feel things deeply.'

And so none but One above knew the scalding tears dropped in secret, and the terrible sinking of heart with which she viewed her future.

Clare went over to see Miss Villars in the afternoon, and after a long talk obtained the post she coveted.

'You know,' she confided to her friend, 'since I have felt so differently about things, I have been longing to do some work for God. It is very pleasant living at home, but it is an idle life, isn't it? With Miss Miller's energy, and Agatha aiding her in all the village work, there is nothing left for me, and I long if I can to influence others for good.'

'I am so thankful to hear you say so, and doubly thankful to think of you being in a position to influence others of your own class. The young people at the convalescent home will be so much more likely to confide in you, and be impressed by what you say, from the very fact of your being young yourself, and not beyond all the innocent pleasures of youth.'

'But,' said Clare depreciatingly, 'I am such a beginner; that is the one thing frightens me—my want of experience. And I am still very moody, Miss Villars. Don't smile; I do think at the bottom of my heart my restlessness and discontent is gone; but some days everything seems black, and I wonder if I am a real Christian after all. I wish I had your feelings.'

'Oh, these feelings!' said Miss Villars, with a little laugh.

'You will be better, my dear child, when your life is more filled up, and you have so much of others' troubles and pleasures to think of, that you will have no time for your own.'

So Clare came back with her future settled, and the sisters were very busy for the next few weeks making preparation for the two departing ones. Alick and his cousin were in and out, and the former seemed to get doubly depressed when he heard that Elfie was going away. Yet up to the last his tongue seemed tied, and it was not until she was actually in the railway carriage that he said a word. He had insisted upon seeing her off, and Agatha, fussing over the luggage, was not aware that anything passed between them.

Holding Elfie's hand tightly in his own, he said huskily and with emphasis:—

'You won't forget me? I shall see you again; and meanwhile, believe I mean it!'

That was all that was said, but the two understood each other, and Elfie leant back in her seat, as the train steamed out of the station, with joy throbbing through her heart.

'I shall not be at Cousin James' long, I am sure,' she repeated over and over to herself; and so bravely and cheerfully she took up her new life, and her letters home were so bright and amusing, that both Agatha and Gwen thought that she was perfectly happy and well.

CHAPTER XVIII

PATTY'S GRAVE

'But when they left her to herself again,
Death, like a friend's voice from a distant field,
Approaching through the darkness, called.'

—Tennyson

The summer came and went very quietly. Gwen remained with Agatha, but was wholly engrossed in her writing. Sometimes Agatha would remonstrate with her, when she came to breakfast looking worn and haggard, and confessing she had been writing in the study till between two and three in the morning.

'You will wear yourself out. Why don't you take it more quietly? There is no need for such labour.'

'You would realize the need if you were in my shoes,' said Gwen, 'and felt your debts hanging over your head every minute of the day. I will never rest until I have repaid all that has been lost.'

'But that will be impossible, and unnecessary.'

Amy Le Feuvre

'I don't think so,' was the curt reply.

Gwen was much up in town, sometimes at the British Museum, and she worked away at Mr. Lester's manuscripts whenever she could spare time from her usual writing. One afternoon she rejoiced Agatha's heart by announcing her intention of taking a walk.

'I shall stroll over to the Howitts. Have you any message for Deb?'

'I think not. I hear that Patty has not been well this last week. You might take her a little pudding. Deb was not working at the vicarage this week because of her illness.'

Gwen set out, and the fresh, keen autumn air refreshed and invigorated her. She found the little cottage nearly hidden from view by the heavily-laden apple trees, but there was a stillness about the place that was not usual. The door was on the latch, and when she stepped inside the kitchen, it was empty.

However, the door leading into the sisters' bedroom was ajar, and Gwen found Patty in bed, and Deb vainly endeavouring to make her swallow a basin of gruel.

'It isn't gruel I'll be wantin', when I know how you burns my best 'namel saucepan in the doin' of it. 'Tis a mercy I've got the honey all in, and now there'll be the apples to be gathered and preserved; and who's to have the doin' of it, wi' you, whose heart and hands are only in the dressmakin', and me a achin' and smartin' wi' pains from head to toe, and worse to foller?'

'Then I'll away to the doctor this blessed minit, and Miss Miller will be for sendin' that parish nurse she's a startin' of, and who's a kickin' up her heels with naught to keep her out o' mischief. She'll be flyin' down here wi' the greatest joy, and will handle your pots and pans as poor me isn't able, and I'll be back to my dressmakin', not being of no manner o' use in tendin' a sick sister, who's that partickler, and full o' fuss—'

Deb stopped here, catching sight of Gwen, and her face brightened as she turned to her.

'Come in, my dear; we're just two quarrelsome old women, as you know, and Patty, poor thing! is a new hand at illness. 'Tis a bad attack o' cold in the innards—flannelation o' the lung, a neighbour thinks; but she be a contrary patient, and she won't have no doctor.'

Gwen stepped up to the invalid, and looked down with pity upon the thin gaunt frame stretched on the tiny bed. Patty's face was flushed, her lips dry and parched, and her eyes feverishly bright. She seemed very talkative.

'Come in, miss, and welcome. Better in here, where I can see things is what they should be, than out in the kitchen, which to my certain knowledge hasn't been cleaned out proper since I took to bed, and that was week ago yesterday. If I could get better, please God, I never would put off the scrubbin' out o' the cupboards agen. Twas Toosday, the day for to do 'em, and I says to myself, "I seem strangely tired, I'll leave it till tomorrow;" and Wednesday found me in my bed, too bad to move, and the cupboards hasn't had their right chance yet, and Deb she be but a poor cleaner. Ay, dearie me, it'll go hard wi' me if I'm not so much as able to wash myself, and— but there, the good Lord will take me home when it comes to that, for when my cleanin' days be over my livin' days will be over too.'

Amy Le Feuvre

'Now look here,' said Gwen authoritatively, 'you are talking yourself into a fever. Lie still, take your gruel, and hear me do the talking. Now, Deb, give me the stuff. It looks delicious. I'll turn nurse.'

There was no resisting Gwen. Patty took it from her hands as meekly as a child, and Deb heaved a deep sigh of relief when she saw the last drop swallowed.

"Tis a great gift to be determined in your will,' she said to Gwen. 'Patty never has had any who could master her. We be both so masterful; that is where all the trouble cometh between us.'

'Determination, or, rather, self will, has been my curse,' said Gwen, with a smile and a sigh.

'Now has it now?' said Deb, leaning her bare elbows on the bed rail, and looking at her with interest. 'Folk do say in the village that you met with a deal o' trouble out in them foreign parts, and some haythen rascal robbed you of all you stood up in. When you come to see us after your return, we kept quiet, not likin' to ask; but Patty says to me when you'd a gone, "She's been through a deal o' trouble, for there be hard lines on her face, and a sad ring in her laugh," and we felt mortal sorry for you, my dear.'

'Tis a good thing to have a will,' said Patty from her pillows, 'so long as it don't get above the Lord's will.'

'That it couldn't never do,' quickly returned Deb; 'for God Almighty can snap a body's will like dry twigs, and He be our Master. 'Tis a blasphemous thing to try to get the better o' our Maker; and Miss Gwen's will be not that sort.'

'I think it has been,' said Gwen, sitting down and softly

stroking one of Patty's withered old hands. 'I thought I could manage my life and everybody else's independent of God, and He has shown me my mistake. It has been a bitter lesson, but I hope I have learnt it.'

There was silence. Something in the simplicity and quaintness of this old couple always drew out Gwen's best feelings, and she spoke to them of things she would never mention to any one else.

'We've heerd say,' said Deb, after a pause, 'that all you young ladies have lost your money. But that, may be, is only a tale.'

'Very close to truth,' said Gwen; 'and my earnest desire is to earn as much money as possible. Can you tell me how to do it?'

'Young ladies set about such things different to us,' said Deb, thoughtfully.

Patty looked up quickly.

'If so be that this is my last sickness, you'll not be long after me, Deb, I'm thinkin', and then what about the golden russet? Will Miss Gwen like to have the use o' it?'

Gwen thought her mind was wandering, until she saw how fearfully Deb looked round the room, as if afraid any neighbour might be within hearing.

'Hush you now! 'Tis not the time to be talkin' of our savin's. Miss Gwen will take no notice o' such talk.'

And Gwen did not, only chatted on till Patty seemed to grow more restless, and then she took her leave. When she told Agatha how she had found them, Agatha at once resolved to send the doctor.

'She may die. So often, when once people like her give up and take to their bed, they never leave it again.'

The doctor went, and thought very gravely of Patty's state. Agatha and Gwen were constant visitors at the cottage, and did much to comfort poor Deb, who, now convinced that her sister might never recover, was overwhelmed with misery.

'We come into the world together, and we're bound to go out together,' she kept repeating; 'it ain't likely as how she'll leave me behind.'

And if a neighbour would assure her that she was well and strong, and likely to survive her sister for many years, she would only shake her head and say, "Tis against nature; and if so be as her days are numbered, then so is mine, and I shall be taken, disease or no disease.'

She went about the cottage in a solemn way, turning out old hoards, writing in crabbed handwriting directions about various matters, and Gwen came upon a scrap of paper one day with the following items:—

Cost of two plain coffins…
Parish clerk's fee ……
Bit of ground by the corner yew.
Bearers for Patty ……
Bearers for Deborah ……

The spaces left she evidently meant to fill up. Gwen promptly burnt the paper, and took her to task about it; but nothing would comfort her, or convince her that by any possibility she could outlive her sister.

And then one evening, quietly and simply, like a little child, Patty passed away. Her last words were to her sister:—

'The good Lord has got me, Deb, and He'll not let me fall.'

Deb sat by her bedside as one stunned. She looked up piti0-fully when Gwen came to her side.

'I'm still here—but I'm just waitin' my call.'

It was with difficulty that she could be induced to eat anything, and when the time came for Patty to be carried to the grave, she saw the little party of mourners set out in stony unconcern.

'They might have let her bide till I were ready to go, too. It'll be a double expense, and I can't be here much longer.'

Gwen's heart went out to the desolate old woman, and she hardly let a day pass without going over to see her. About a week after, she went one afternoon, but found the house closed. The stillness and desertion of the cottage sent a thrill of fear through her. Fearing that Deb's mind had become slightly unhinged, she wondered if she had destroyed her own life. She tried the door, but it was locked; and then she noticed a piece of paper tucked into the sill. Taking it out, she read:—

'If you be Miss Gwen, the key is under the water butt; if you be any other body, let it be. Deb.'

Gwen took the key up, unlocked the door, and went in. The kitchen was spotlessly clean, the grate shining with blacklead. On the square deal table lay a letter with her name upon it. But before reading it, Gwen hastily searched the house, to make certain that it was empty, and then she perused the badly written epistle.

'Miss Gwen,—

'Your humble servant Deborah Howlitt write these lines to
you hoping it may find you as it leaves her at present
knowing your kind heart, and I always did have a leaning
towards you more than most, and so did Patty for her said
you were a woman of good understanding I think it best
to leave you all our savings which you will find under our
golden russet in my mother's china tea-pot, for Patty said
the same when she were a dying. And you will use them
to save you from the House if your money has gone from
you. Will you be so good as to give the clothes in our
chest of drawers to them that need them. We did think of
turning our brown serges, and if they were ripped round
the bottom and braided afresh would be good Sunday
skirts. I have been to our grave three nights running for I
heard her calling, but the good God won't take me yet. I'm
going to-night, and may be I shall not be back. Patty
could not say I have not cleaned for there is no speck of
dirt to be seen. And now goodbye and never put your will
against the Almighty for I am praying not to do it myself
for I am a poor old desolate woman and if He says "Live,"
I will live, but He seems to say to-night "Come," and,—

"Just as I am, without one plea,
But that Thy blood was shed for me,
And that Thou bidst me come to Thee,
O Lamb of God, I come!"

'Your obedient servant,
'DEBORAH HOWLITT.'

Gwen hurriedly left the cottage after reading this, and went
straight to the churchyard. No one evidently had been near

Patty's grave that day, for there, lying in long grass, with her arms crossed on the uncovered mound, and her grey head bowed upon them, was the cold, stiff form of poor Deb. How many hours she had been there in the still coldness of an October's night no one could tell; but the doctor put down her death to grief and exposure. Gwen broke the tidings to Agatha with a sob in her voice.

'I loved those old women. They were the only friends I had here.'

CHAPTER XIX

THE RIGHTFUL HEIR

And words of true love pass from tongue to tongue,
As singing birds from one bough to another.'
—*Longfellow*

When Gwen had the savings of the old women dug up from the roots of their favourite apple-tree, she found to her amazement that no less than 95 pounds had been put away in the old teapot, and for some time she hesitated about appropriating it.

Miss Miller came round to advise, for she was most excited about it all.

'I have been making inquiries, my dear, about their relatives as if you feel any qualms about taking their savings, I thought you would be glad to hear of their next-of-kin. But they seem to have no one left belonging to them. A friend of mine in this neighbourhood was left 300 pounds by an old nurse once. She founded a parish room and club with it, and I need not say that if you wish to give it away in charity, I shall be very glad to advise you. I said to Wilfrid that I did not believe you would keep it yourself, for though tales have been flying about that you and your two younger sisters have lost your money, I can see that you are not destitute. You still keep a very good table, for Mrs. Stone tells me she supplies you with poultry and eggs, and is not able to sell me her fowls under 2s. 6d; as she says you always give a fair price for your things.'

'I have quite made up my mind about the way in which I shall use it, Miss Miller,' said Gwen, trying hard to speak politely.

There was never any love lost between that good lady and herself, and Agatha dreaded every encounter between them.

'On some pet charity of your own?'

'You may call it so, if you like;' and nothing more would Gwen say on the subject.

Later on, she told Agatha she would send it straight to Walter.

'He is on my mind dreadfully. Not one word of reproach did he ever give me, and I am thankful I can help him this much. It is more of a charity to give it to him than let it drift through Miss Miller's fingers. What an odious woman she is!'

'Oh, hush! I can't bear to hear you talk so. She has no tact, and makes many blunders, but is really thoroughly kind at heart. I never mind her speeches. I don't think any one does who really knows her. But I am very glad you are sending it out to Walter, and I shall be able to add a little to it when you do so. Our expenses are very small now, and if you will not let me spend any on yourself, I shall gladly send it abroad.'

Amy Le Feuvre

'How well old Nannie's text has fitted into your life!' said Gwen, musing: '"Trust in the Lord, and do good, . . . and verily thou shalt be fed." You have proved that promise true, for you are the only one of us all that is provided for life.'

I think we have all been cared for so far,' said Agatha quietly. 'You will find your verse no less true than mine: "Commit thy way unto the Lord, trust also in Him, and He shall bring it to pass."'

Gwen was silent. She could not talk freely about her feelings to any one, but she had, as she expressed it to Deb, 'learnt her lesson.' Her self-confidence had been shaken to the roots, and she was no longer desirous of following her own plans to the exclusion of all advice from others. Having discovered that she could make mistakes, she began to wonder whether her life had not been full of them; and the gradual conviction of this drove her to her knees, and led her to the feet of the great Teacher as a little child.

One evening, soon after poor Deb's death, Agatha and Gwen were sitting down to a cosy evening together, when they were surprised by the sudden entrance of Alick Lester. He seemed strangely perturbed, and very anxious to pour out his trouble into Agatha's ears. When Gwen made a movement to go, he begged her to remain.

'You will all know it soon. It will be no secret, but I'd give a good deal to have prevented it coming out now. May I begin from the beginning?'

Then, taking a seat, he plunged into it at once.

'You know I found some papers in my father's cupboard. He knew of them, but had never given me a hint of it, except that he had made me promise to be home if possible last autumn. It appears that my grandfather before he died made a codicil to his will, and handed it over to the keeping of my father, forbidding him to ever show it to any one, until the right time came to act upon it. I suppose the poor old man may have wished to right matters a little, and had got over his bitterness about my father's marriage. I know he took a good deal of notice of me as a small boy, but I never dreamt he had any special reason for it. The codicil simply transferred the whole of his property from the hands of my uncle to myself when I should reach my twenty-sixth year. This I did last September, and this accounts for my father's anxiety to have me back at that time. It appears now that my uncle's valet got wind of this—how, and where, I can't imagine—but he told my uncle he knew my father held some important papers in his hands that concerned him. And after my father's death, as you know, Miss Dane, my uncle came down here to try and get hold of them. Well, after our return, I suppose the delight of having Roger back again put the whole affair out of my uncle's head, but lately he hasn't been very well—at least that is the most charitable way to look at it—and he has been perpetually nagging at me about the contents of the cupboard, and asking to see them.'

'I cannot think why you did not show them at once to him,' interrupted Agatha.

The young fellow looked a little confused.

'I daresay you may think me an ass, but I could not for the life of me bear the thought of turning the old man out after all these years. He hasn't got many more years to live, and has seemed so perfectly secure in his possession that I hadn't the heart to show the codicil to him. Of course, I know most people would call me a fool—our old lawyer practically did so—but I put off doing anything about it, as much for the sake of Roger, perhaps, as his father.

Amy Le Feuvre

'Well, last night I lost my temper, and when my uncle began to attack my father's good name, and hint that he had dishonourably kept family papers from the head of the family, I whipped out the codicil in his face, and asked him to read it through. Of course there was an awful row. At first he thought I had forged it, and he telegraphed to his lawyer, who came down the first thing this morning, and we had a great consultation in the library. Then my uncle shut himself up in his room, and has refused to see me since. I don't know how it will all end. I have begged and implored Roger to persuade him to stay on, and let things be as they were; but he won't hear of it, and meditates leaving at once. I feel awfully low about it, but what can I do?'

'You are a very quixotic young man,' said Gwen, unable to keep from smiling at the woe-begone face in front of her. 'You should be thankful it's all out, and your uncle knows the truth.'

'Yes, and to a certain extent I am. But I don't want them to clear out, and leave me in possession. I never expected to be a rich man, and don't altogether like the idea of settling down here.'

Gwen laughed again, and left the room, saying, 'You shouldn't quarrel with good fortune when it comes to you.'

For a moment there was silence, then Alick turned to Agatha a little awkwardly, a blush coming to his bronzed cheeks.

'Miss Dane, do you know my one comfort in all this? It is thinking that now I have a right to speak to your sister.'

'To Elfie?' asked Agatha.

'Yes, I am sure you won't raise an objection, will you? I

know I'm not half good enough for her; but if she'll only listen to me, I feel as if life will be too good to live.'

And for the next half-hour Agatha listened to a flow of eloquence on Elfie's perfections, which amused and yet touched her, for it showed her how deeply devoted the young man was in his love.

Major Lester was not long in leaving the Hall. He announced his intention of travelling abroad with his son, and before a month was gone Alick was left alone. The cousins parted with mutual regret. Roger took the blow to his future prospects bravely and manfully, and told Alick that he looked forward to see his bride at the Hall very soon.

And then, one day, without a word to any one, Alick travelled down to Dane Hall.

Elfie had been having a trying time—a time that tested all her powers of cheerfulness to carry her through it. Mrs. Dane was confined to her room with bronchitis, not ill enough to lie still and leave the responsibility of her household to Elfie, but perpetually questioning the girl's management, and giving contrary orders to the servants, who were all in a state of irritation and turbulence. Mr. Dane was impatient of the slightest hitch in the domestic machinery, and, now that his wife was too indisposed to hear his complaints, vented all his ill-humour upon his young cousin.

But Elfie's sunny temper did not forsake her; and if, in the privacy of her own room, home-sickness and loneliness got the better of her at times, she always preserved a cheerful front in public, and earnestly strove, not only to do her duty, but to be happy in doing it, and to make those around her happy too.

Amy Le Feuvre

It was a bright, spring afternoon, when, at last relieved from attendance on the invalid, Elfie took her hat and went out into the garden to enjoy the fresh air and sunshine. She was singing away to herself and gathering some jonquils for the dinner-table, when she was joined by her cousin James.

'Elfrida, I am told that neither of the carriage horses can be taken out. It is extraordinary that with four horses doing hardly anything there should be this constant difficulty in getting one of them to drive.'

'Yes,' said Elfie a little carelessly, 'I have always heard that the more horses you have the less work you get out of them. Where do you want to go, Cousin James? Can't you take Firefly in the dog-cart?'

'It does not matter to you where I wish to go. I wish to drive the pair, and I am convinced this new groom is an utterly incompetent man. Ever since we have been in this house we have had a perpetual change of servants, and I was in hopes that when you came it would be different.'

'I am not responsible for your grooms. I have nothing to do with them,' said Elfie brightly. 'I should ask Fenton what he think of this new groom.'

'Fenton is insufferable with his insolent bearing and behaviour, and you encourage him in his familiarity. I heard you were taking tea with him and his wife yesterday. I must beg you never to do such a thing again as long as you are under my roof.'

'You must remember, Cousin James, Fenton has known us all since we were tiny children. He gave us our first riding lessons, and Aunt Mildred treated him very differently to most of the servants. He lived with her for forty years, he was telling me.'

'I don't wish for any arguments, if I give you an order. I think you sometimes forget your position with us. You are here to relieve your cousin Helen of all worry and anxiety about household matters, and it has been a great disappointment to us both that you seem incapable of keeping things straight. I hear that the cook is leaving, and has been exceedingly insolent to your cousin, telling her that she will not have two mistresses. I do not wish to interfere in these matters, but I must request you to make more effort to maintain the discipline necessary in such a large household.'

Elfie was so accustomed to these daily grumblings that she went on picking her flowers in silence; the brightness of the day seemed already clouded for her, and she gave an involuntary sigh, as after a little further complaining her cousin walked away.

'They have it all, wealth and comfort all round them; and yet are two discontented, miserable people. I wouldn't exchange places with them for all the world.'

'A gentleman in the drawing-room has called to see you, miss.'

It was the footman brought the message.

Elfie started, flushed, and then went into the house to meet her fate. There was only one person it could be, and her instinct told her that life would be different after this interview to what it was at present. Her time of uncertainty and waiting was now at an end, and Dane Hall would soon be her home no more.

Amy Le Feuvre

CHAPTER XX

BROUGHT BACK

'Far, far above thy thought
His wisdom shall appear,
When fully He this work hath wrought,
That caused thy needless fear!'

Three months later. Jasmine Cottage was full of lively voices and laughter. Clare and Elfie were both at home, the former for a month's holiday, and the latter till she left it to take up her quarters in the Hall as bride and mistress. Alick was there, with no cloud upon his brow, and full of eager anticipation of all that he was going to do upon the estate in the future; and Agatha and Clare looked on at the young couple with interest and sympathy. They were gathered together in the verandah, and Gwen only was absent. Alick presently asked for her.

'She has gone to London to her publishers. You will be interested to know, Alick, that it is about your father's manuscripts. Gwen has finished them at last, and it is to consult about bringing them out, that she has gone. We expect her back every moment.'

Agatha looked along the road as she spoke, and Alick's eyes followed her gaze.

'Here she comes; I know her walk!' he exclaimed. 'Rapid, defiant, and indifferent to all around!'

'You shall not talk of her like that,' remonstrated Elfie, 'and it isn't true of her.'

'I admire her awfully, only I'm just a little bit afraid of her.'

'I don't believe you're afraid of any one!'

Here Gwen appeared on the scene. She seemed flushed and rather perturbed.

'Have I got my business done satisfactorily? Yes, I hope I have. Agatha, I am famishing; have you got anything for me to eat? That's right. I will go straight into the dining-room now.'

Agatha followed her in.

'You look tired out. Sit down, and I will pour you out a cup of coffee. I expected you back earlier.'

'I was detained.'

For a few minutes there was silence. Then Gwen leant back in her chair and regarded Agatha with serious eyes.

'You're a safe old thing. I think I can trust you,' she said. 'First of all tell me, do you think Clare happy now?'

'I have never known her so happy in her life before,' said Agatha, wondering at Gwen's tone. 'Of course, I know she has her sad times, but she is far sweeter and even-tempered than she used to be. Miss Villars was telling me the other day, she has found her niche exactly. All the visitors at the Convalescent Home are loud in their praise other, and I really think her heart is in it.'

'Then it would be a pity to disturb her.'

'What do you mean?'

'Well, the fact is, I heard in town to-day rumours about Hugh turning up at some mission station in Africa. People say he was never killed after all. I went to the Foreign Office about it. They know for certain it is some English officer, but cannot be sure it is Hugh.'

'Oh, Gwen!'

Agatha seemed too dazed by the news to say more at first.

'We must keep it to ourselves for the present. It would be dreadful for her if it proved a false report,' continued Gwen; 'and really, she seems so resigned now, that one dreads the effect of such news upon her. Do you think she ever really cared for him? I have my doubts. I remember how restless, and discontented she used to be when he was alive; and look at the change in her now!'

'Yes,' said Agatha quietly; 'but the change is not due to his death, Gwen. Clare has found out for herself the truth of Nannie's verse for her. She was always restless until she came to the Rest-giver, and now she is at peace. Circumstances do not sway her as they used to do.'

'Well,' said Gwen, after a slight pause, 'I hope it may be true, if she really loves him. It is like a story-book, the long-lost lover come to life again! Don't say a word to any one. They have promised to send us the first information they receive.'

For the next few days both Agatha and Gwen appeared to the others very restless and pre-occupied; but as a week or two passed away without further tidings, they tried to banish it from their thoughts, and in a measure succeeded.

Gwen was delighted at the prospects of her book coming out, and hoped to realize a good sum from it, more than she at one time could have thought possible to be earned by her pen. And when, a little later, she received the first instalment of it, she sent a cheque straight out to Meta Seton.

'I feel convinced,' she confided to Agatha, 'that she still cares for Walter; and it is only her father that has insisted upon her breaking it off. I should be so thankful if they came together again. In Walter's last letter he mentions having met her, and I think that they may have arrived at a secret understanding with one another; he writes in much better spirits.'

'If she is a wife worth having, she would never desert him for his poverty,' said Agatha.

Gwen shook her head and sighed, for she knew the world better than simple-minded Agatha did. But her writing took her mind off the startling news she had heard, and Agatha was equally engrossed in preparing Elfie's trousseau, so that though they were always on the watch for any news in the papers, they did not mention the subject to one another, and it was a distinct shock to Agatha to receive a telegram one morning.

'Captain Hugh Knox alive. Coming home. Break it to his friends.'

Amy Le Feuvre

Clare was doing some work for Elfie when the telegram arrived. Agatha hastily consulted Gwen in the study, and then came into the dining-room, where the two younger girls were sitting.

'Who is the telegram from?' asked Elfie quickly. 'We have so few here that Clare and I are quite curious about it.'

Agatha sat down, and her hands trembled as she unfolded and refolded the yellow envelope in her grasp.

'It contains very strange news,' she said slowly 'wonderfully strange, and I don't quite know how to tell it to you.'

Both Clare and Elfie dropped their work instantly, for they saw her agitation.

'Not bad news?' exclaimed Clare.

'No; very, very good news for you, Clare.'

Clare's cheeks grew pale at once.

'Oh, Agatha, speak out; don't keep us in suspense any longer!'

And then Agatha said as quietly as she could:

'It is about Hugh, Clare. Can you bear it? He was never killed, after all, and this is to say that he is coming home.'

Clare did not faint, nor call out, nor did she utter a word. Only the quick blood rushing to her cheeks, and then as quickly ebbing from them, showed that she was moved at all. Motionless she sat, staring out of the window as if she were in a dream. Then at last she spoke.

'Oh, Agatha, I shall never forgive you if it is not true!'

The vehement intensity of her tone drew Agatha to her side at once. Stooping over her she kissed her. 'My darling Clare, it is true. Thank God with all your heart that it is so!'

And then in a few minutes a burst of tears relieved the overcharged brain, and Clare fled to her room, there to thank on her knees for such unlooked-for joy.

The days that followed were trying ones, but Clare bore them well. She went to see her lover's family, and it was there in the Yorkshire home that she met the long-lost one again.

Captain Knox seemed but a shadow of his former self. Fever and privations had told upon him, and Clare shuddered when she heard his story. For many months he had been kept captive amongst the native tribe that had taken him and his comrades by surprise in the bush. He was subject to much cruelty and many indignities, but at last managed to make his escape, and for some months lived in the thick forests, striving to find his way back to civilization. At last he was found by a missionary, almost at the point of death, and tenderly nursed back to health and strength at a small mission station. It was some time, however, before he could send tidings of his escape, and long before he was well enough to be brought down to the coast. He had much to tell to Clare, and also much to hear.

'I cannot believe it is really you,' she said to him, when alone with him one day; 'I keep wondering if I shall wake up and find it all a dream.'

'You had become accustomed to live without me, had you?' he said, smiling. 'Would you rather I had not come back to disturb your life again? You seem to be so happy in your present work.'

'Oh, Hugh, if you only knew what I have gone through, you would not talk so! I don't think you have been out of my thoughts for a single day. God has helped me to bear your loss, but I never knew how your life was woven into mine, till the awful news came that I had lost you!'

'We will not think about it,' said Captain Knox, with deep feeling. 'We have been brought together again, thank God, and I believe we are both the better for what we have suffered. It is wonderful to see the way that we are led, and the goodness and love that brings sweet out of bitter, and blessing out of evil.'

'And,' said Clare softly, as she leaned her head against his shoulder, and felt the support of his strong arm round her, 'we have both been drawn inside the kingdom, Hugh. That is the best of all. We will serve our Master together, and not death itself can separate us now.'

One more scene before we leave the four sisters. Nannie is the conspicuous figure in it. She has been brought to Jasmine Cottage, and it is the eve of Elfie's marriage. The girls were gathered round her in the cosy bedroom that had been prepared for her, and they were full of mirth and happiness.

Gwen had been astonishing them by a piece of news that she had been keeping to herself for a long time, and this was that she had at last listened to Clement Arkwright, and was engaged to him.

'They say that if one wedding comes off in a family, others are sure to follow,' she said, by way of excusing herself; 'and he has been bothering my life out lately. I never seem to go up to town without tumbling across him somewhere. I think I have no spirit left to resist him as I used to do. But one thing I have told him, and that is that he will have to wait till I have cleared off more of my debts.'

'You have no debts,' said Agatha; 'it is nonsense to talk like that.'

'I shall never lift up my head and breathe freely till I have at any rate returned Walter his money,' said Gwen very emphatically.

'Ay, my dear,' put in Nannie affectionately; 'we'd rather your head weren't lifted just yet. 'Tis apt to rear itself a little too high, and 'tis the bowed head that gets the blessing of the Lord.'

'Nannie,' said Elfie impulsively, 'say our verses to us again, will you? Do you remember when you gave them to us? Put your hands on our heads as you used to do when we were little children, and we will receive them again as your blessing.'

And this Nannie did; and as she repeated the beautiful words, each sister confessed in the depths of her heart what a blessing they had been to her.

'Trust in the Lord and do good, so shalt thou dwell in the land, and verily thou shalt be fed.'

'Delight thyself also in the Lord, and He shall give thee the desires of thine heart.'

'Commit thy way unto the Lord, trust also in Him, and He shall bring it to pass.'

'Rest in the Lord, and wait patiently for Him.... Those that

Amy Le Feuvre

wait upon the Lord, they shall inherit the earth.'

'And,' said Agatha, 'the key-note to that Psalm is, "Fret not." We thought it a terrible blow when Cousin James defrauded us of our rights; but how wonderfully we have been cared for since!'

'Even when I did my best to ruin the whole lot of you,' put in Gwen.

And then Nannie repeated the last verse of her favourite Psalm:

'And the Lord shall help them and deliver them: He shall deliver them from the wicked, and save them because they trust in Him.'

FINIS

Choose from Thousands of 1stWorldLibrary Classics By

A. M. Barnard	Booth Tarkington	Edward Everett Hale
Ada Leverson	Boyd Cable	Edward J. O'Biren
Adolphus William Ward	Bram Stoker	Edward S. Ellis
Aesop	C. Collodi	Edwin L. Arnold
Agatha Christie	C. E. Orr	Eleanor Atkins
Alexander Aaronsohn	C. M. Ingleby	Eleanor Hallowell Abbott
Alexander Kielland	Carolyn Wells	Eliot Gregory
Alexandre Dumas	Catherine Parr Traill	Elizabeth Gaskell
Alfred Gatty	Charles A. Eastman	Elizabeth McCracken
Alfred Ollivant	Charles Amory Beach	Elizabeth Von Arnim
Alice Duer Miller	Charles Dickens	Ellem Key
Alice Turner Curtis	Charles Dudley Warner	Emerson Hough
Alice Dunbar	Charles Farrar Browne	Emilie F. Carlen
Allen Chapman	Charles Ives	Emily Bronte
Alleyne Ireland	Charles Kingsley	Emily Dickinson
Ambrose Bierce	Charles Klein	Enid Bagnold
Amelia E. Barr	Charles Hanson Towne	Enilor Macartney Lane
Amory H. Bradford	Charles Lathrop Pack	Erasmus W. Jones
Andrew Lang	Charles Romyn Dake	Ernie Howard Pie
Andrew McFarland Davis	Charles Whibley	Ethel May Dell
Andy Adams	Charles Willing Beale	Ethel Turner
Angela Brazil	Charlotte M. Braeme	Ethel Watts Mumford
Anna Alice Chapin	Charlotte M. Yonge	Eugene Sue
Anna Sewell	Charlotte Perkins Stetson	Eugenie Foa
Annie Besant	Clair W. Hayes	Eugene Wood
Annie Hamilton Donnell	Clarence Day Jr.	Eustace Hale Ball
Annie Payson Call	Clarence E. Mulford	Evelyn Everett-green
Annie Roe Carr	Clemence Housman	Everard Cotes
Annonaymous	Confucius	F. H. Cheley
Anton Chekhov	Coningsby Dawson	F. J. Cross
Archibald Lee Fletcher	Cornelis DeWitt Wilcox	F. Marion Crawford
Arnold Bennett	Cyril Burleigh	Fannie E. Newberry
Arthur C. Benson	D. H. Lawrence	Federick Austin Ogg
Arthur Conan Doyle	Daniel Defoe	Ferdinand Ossendowski
Arthur M. Winfield	David Garnett	Fergus Hume
Arthur Ransome	Dinah Craik	Florence A. Kilpatrick
Arthur Schnitzler	Don Carlos Janes	Fremont B. Deering
Arthur Train	Donald Keyhoe	Francis Bacon
Atticus	Dorothy Kilner	Francis Darwin
B.H. Baden-Powell	Dougan Clark	Frances Hodgson Burnett
B. M. Bower	Douglas Fairbanks	Frances Parkinson Keyes
B. C. Chatterjee	E. Nesbit	Frank Gee Patchin
Baroness Emmuska Orczy	E. P. Roe	Frank Harris
Baroness Orczy	E. Phillips Oppenheim	Frank Jewett Mather
Basil King	E. S. Brooks	Frank L. Packard
Bayard Taylor	Earl Barnes	Frank V. Webster
Ben Macomber	Edgar Rice Burroughs	Frederic Stewart Isham
Bertha Muzzy Bower	Edith Van Dyne	Frederick Trevor Hill
Bjornstjerne Bjornson	Edith Wharton	Frederick Winslow Taylor

Friedrich Kerst
Friedrich Nietzsche
Fyodor Dostoyevsky
G.A. Henty
G.K. Chesterton
Gabrielle E. Jackson
Garrett P. Serviss
Gaston Leroux
George A. Warren
George Ade
Geroge Bernard Shaw
George Cary Eggleston
George Durston
George Ebers
George Eliot
George Gissing
George MacDonald
George Meredith
George Orwell
George Sylvester Viereck
George Tucker
George W. Cable
George Wharton James
Gertrude Atherton
Gordon Casserly
Grace E. King
Grace Gallatin
Grace Greenwood
Grant Allen
Guillermo A. Sherwell
Gulielma Zollinger
Gustav Flaubert
H. A. Cody
H. B. Irving
H. C. Bailey
H. G. Wells
H. H. Munro
H. Irving Hancock
H. R. Naylor
H. Rider Haggard
H. W. C. Davis
Haldeman Julius
Hall Caine
Hamilton Wright Mabie
Hans Christian Andersen
Harold Avery
Harold McGrath
Harriet Beecher Stowe
Harry Castlemon
Harry Coghill
Harry Houidini

Hayden Carruth
Helent Hunt Jackson
Helen Nicolay
Hendrik Conscience
Hendy David Thoreau
Henri Barbusse
Henrik Ibsen
Henry Adams
Henry Ford
Henry Frost
Henry James
Henry Jones Ford
Henry Seton Merriman
Henry W Longfellow
Herbert A. Giles
Herbert Carter
Herbert N. Casson
Herman Hesse
Hildegard G. Frey
Homer
Honore De Balzac
Horace B. Day
Horace Walpole
Horatio Alger Jr.
Howard Pyle
Howard R. Garis
Hugh Lofting
Hugh Walpole
Humphry Ward
Ian Maclaren
Inez Haynes Gillmore
Irving Bacheller
Isabel Cecilia Williams
Isabel Hornibrook
Israel Abrahams
Ivan Turgenev
J. G.Austin
J. Henri Fabre
J. M. Barrie
J. M. Walsh
J. Macdonald Oxley
J. R. Miller
J. S. Fletcher
J. S. Knowles
J. Storer Clouston
J. W. Duffield
Jack London
Jacob Abbott
James Allen
James Andrews
James Baldwin

James Branch Cabell
James DeMille
James Joyce
James Lane Allen
James Lane Allen
James Oliver Curwood
James Oppenheim
James Otis
James R. Driscoll
Jane Abbott
Jane Austen
Jane L. Stewart
Janet Aldridge
Jens Peter Jacobsen
Jerome K. Jerome
Jessie Graham Flower
John Buchan
John Burroughs
John Cournos
John F. Kennedy
John Gay
John Glasworthy
John Habberton
John Joy Bell
John Kendrick Bangs
John Milton
John Philip Sousa
John Taintor Foote
Jonas Lauritz Idemil Lie
Jonathan Swift
Joseph A. Altsheler
Joseph Carey
Joseph Conrad
Joseph E. Badger Jr
Joseph Hergesheimer
Joseph Jacobs
Jules Vernes
Julian Hawthrone
Julie A Lippmann
Justin Huntly McCarthy
Kakuzo Okakura
Karle Wilson Baker
Kate Chopin
Kenneth Grahame
Kenneth McGaffey
Kate Langley Bosher
Kate Langley Bosher
Katherine Cecil Thurston
Katherine Stokes
L. A. Abbot
L. T. Meade

www.ingramcontent.com/pod-product-compliance
Lightning Source LLC
Chambersburg PA
CBHW030323180626
46810CB00003B/1210